# The History of
# Speed

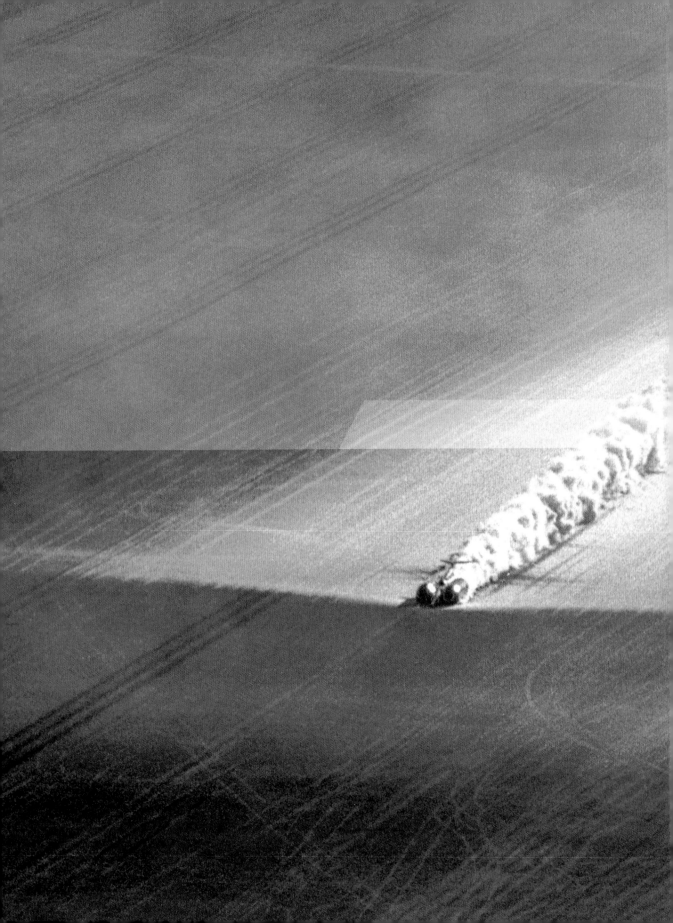

# The History of
# Speed
*by Martin Roach*

**SIMON &
SCHUSTER**

London · New York · Sydney · Toronto · New Delhi

MMXX

*Dedicated to Jessi Combs*

# Contents

# Foreword

'If I have to explain why we are doing this – you will never understand.' As usual, ThrustSSC driver Andy Green hit the nail on the head. Why was the ThrustSSC website the largest in the world in 1997, why did literally thousands of people take part in the electronic fundraiser which finally got the ThrustSSC team to Black Rock? It can't possibly be about one man's obsession – there has to be much, much more to land speed racing and to speed.

We live in a risk-averse world – whilst extraordinary achievements are being made with electrons and synthetic biology, they lack the sheer raw team spirit and personal risk of pushing the world speed record into speed regions which are unknown. The visual image of the high speed achievement is so divorced from current lifetime experience that the extraordinary image remains with the viewer for all time. It is easy to surmise that everyone has their personal ambition to leave a tombstone legacy – perhaps not to drive a supersonic LSR car, but at least to have a claim to have been a part of such a massive team achievement.

The 1000 mph Bloodhound project took this to extraordinary levels of public benefit. Einstein had explained that the biggest hindrance to his learning was his education: current technology had advanced so quickly in his lifetime that he was constantly updating his early educational knowledge. There is a valid argument that today's educational process should make the latest educational experience immediately available to schoolchildren – and this is what Bloodhound sought to achieve by

*Richard Noble and his team celebrating breaking the land speed record on 4 October 1983, when Thrust2 hit 633.47 mph.*

making the experience and project understanding available to millions of schoolchildren in 200 countries.

We believe that such enthusiastic interest or inspiration leads to personal aspiration and enhanced educational focus. And there is plenty of precedent – back in the 1960s the US Apollo moon programme spawned a dramatic increase in STEM PhDs in the USA and most probably across the world.

*Richard Noble*

# Author's Note

It is fair to say that the modern world celebrates speed – not just in terms of vehicles and travel, but in nearly every facet of life: rushing to work, walking up quick escalators or shooting up skyscrapers in record-breaking elevators to get to meetings to write fast reports and 'make a quick buck', earning a fast-track promotion to qualify for instant credit card decisions or quick mortgages, spending that fast cash on same-day delivery items, next-day returns, fast food, fast diets, fast fashion, speed dating, instant fame ... speed is everywhere. In modern life, speed is a positive, a preferred state of being, a desirable commodity.

It was speed that opened up modern society, shrunk the globe and eventually, via the internet, opened up the world at the click of a mouse. Consequently, there is now a haste to how we receive information, scrolling, liking and clicking as quickly as allowed by our broadband (a personal slice of the information superhighway that will have been sold to us on the basis of its speed). Popular culture also champions this rapidity, and is inseminated with fast car chases, fast action, fast adverts, fast music, fast lyrics ... we are essentially taught to embrace speed by a society that is obsessed with doing things quickly. Even a leisurely reading of

a weekend edition of *The New York Times* presents us with more information than a thirteenth-century person would have been exposed to in a lifetime. Psychologists and counsellors quote one of the biggest single reasons given for why people need their help is: 'I never have enough time.' In George Simmel's *The Metropolis and Modern Life*, the writer goes as far as to state that speed has challenged time as the prime mover of modern life. There is a certain irony that, as the world gets ever quicker, many people feel they are never moving fast enough.

Set against this cultural backdrop, this book is a chronicle of the cars, land speed vehicles and, perhaps above all, the *characters* who find moving at high speed so utterly invigorating. Time and again, there are tales of speed that are most remarkable for the human narrative rather than the miles per hour on the time sheet. This book is not just about a foot-to-the-floor mentality and top speed records. Speed as a furnace of glamour, as well as its ability to bestow celebrity status, is a crucial part of the tale. The technological advances that speed has bequeathed on both automobile manufacture and society in general are also pivotal. Likewise, the gender of speed and the complex psychology of moving quickly are subjective but essential elements of the story. Necessarily, as this is absolutely not an attempt to glamorize speed, the dark side of the experience is also discussed. Finally, it must be noted that across all these historical accounts are a multitude of evolutions in society and culture, significant moments of note that have all been indelibly affected by speed.

Also, to clarify the parameters of this study, I have chronicled the active experience of speed where it is pursued as a thrill or achievement rather than a commute or base practicality. When you ask someone, 'What is the fastest you have ever been?' they will invariably mention a speed reached in a car or on a motorbike; yet if they have been in an aeroplane, then the answer is more in the region of 500 mph. However, that is a passive experience, and as such is an example of the types of speed that fall outside the criteria of this book.

I would like to add one personal note by way of explanation: cars are my passion, so that is the prism through which I view speed; therefore this book is focused on cars or car-based vehicles, with a few necessary diversions into the world of water speed records and also motorbikes (the latter justifying a stand-alone study).

As I was completing the writing of this book in the summer of 2019, within the space of a few weeks two very significant moments in the history of speed occurred. On 27 August 2019, the fastest female on four wheels, the racer and TV personality Jessi Combs, was killed in a horrific crash in a desert in Oregon, trying to beat her own speed record and possibly eclipse the long-standing overall women's record of 512 mph set back in 1976. Jessi was due to be interviewed for this book, having become my friend in 2017 when she stayed at my home with her pals on a visit to the UK. The shock of her death was deeply felt around the world of speed.

The tragic and long list of fatal incidents in the pursuit of speed illustrates that travelling across the surface of the earth at ballistic speeds is inherently and extremely dangerous - yet there is a seemingly endless queue of people lining up to take speed to the next level, sometimes at an horrific cost.

Yet at the start of the very same month, the Bugatti Chiron had become the first ever road car to pass 300 mph, when their test driver Andy Wallace hit 304.77 mph at VW's Ehra-Lessien test track. The very fact this speed attempt was sanctioned by the biggest car company in the world suggests high speed still has relevance - at least to some - and the way the internet lit up when the news broke, with millions of tweets and reposts within minutes of the news becoming common knowledge, indicates that, to millions of people around the globe, speed matters.

# Chapter 1

# A Pre-History of
# Speed

*The world is moving so fast these days that the man who says it can't be done is generally interrupted by someone doing it.*

American author and poet Elbert Hubbard

In the natural world, speed is perennially vital as an essential tool of survival. Basic anthropology suggests that any creature which can run faster than its peers is less likely to be caught and eaten by predators; conversely, Darwin states that predators which run, attack, hunt and kill faster evolve more successfully. Congruent with these evolutionary facts, the human experience of speed was limited to how fast a person could run, at least prior to the use of animals and the invention of the wheel around 7000 years ago. Someone who could run faster was perceived as more of an alpha individual. This primal fact sets out speed as an evolutionary advantage across the species.

*This ornate vehicle design by Jean Hautsch dates back as far as 1649.*

After these bipedal beginnings, for thousands of years the only way for people to experience faster speeds was using other species as a mode of transport. The earliest known examples of sitting astride animals came on camels, donkeys and horses around 4000 BC. Obviously, the speed of such animals is relatively modest – even though a modern-day thoroughbred race horse might reach 40 mph, such athletic equine performance was not commonplace centuries ago. Also, for a journey of any great distance, horses would need to stop, eat and rest, so even a swift steed might only average around 5 mph on a longer trek. That said, there was an assumption that speed was desirable even back then because, from the earliest times of horses being a primary mode of transport, they were bred to be stronger and faster.

The first known use of wheels can be placed in Iraq around 3500 BC, but in terms of transport (aside from horses), it was early canoes, and then sailing boats in Egypt around 3100 BC, that offered the quickest choices for centuries, particularly with evolving civilizations based around coasts, ports and rivers. Even then, the faster vessels were used to carry goods quickly rather than for the sake of speed alone, and were, of course, restricted to the route and extent of each respective waterway.

The word 'car' can be traced back to the 1300s, derived from a Celtic word similar to 'karra', used to describe a horse-drawn vehicle. By the fourteenth century, historic records contain examples of windmills being strapped to a set of wheels in the hope of travelling on land more swiftly. The seventeenth-century Chinese Emperor Kangxi is said to have commissioned a Belgian missionary to build a steam-powered toy 'car', although this was more for entertainment than travel. It wasn't until the advent of mechanically assisted propulsion that the modern experience of speed began to evolve.

Carriages without horses actually pre-date the first motor car by over a century. The Frenchman Nicholas Joseph Cugnot experimented with steam-powered, self-propelled vehicles in the mid-eighteenth century, albeit with limited success; forty years later, the Englishman Richard Trevithick pioneered his London Steam Carriage, which understandably bemused bystanders in the streets of the English capital in 1803, reaching a dizzying speed of 8.4 mph with eight passengers on board. These early attempts at replacing the horse as a chief means of transport were most often foiled by the sheer weight of the steam engines which, although potentially powerful, were essentially a form of cumbersome static technology that had originally been designed for stationary use in the factories and workshops of the Industrial Revolution. In fact, Trevithick ultimately failed to find investment to develop his idea and eventually sold his engine to a man who immediately stripped the mobile machine and installed the power plant in a mill.

*Arguably one of the first ever 'concept vehicles' – the 1833 three-wheeled steam coach designed by a Dr Church. Said to seat 50 people, this enormous, heavily decorated vehicle was entirely impractical.*

This deeply unreliable early propulsion technology also used massive wooden wheels with iron tyres, which made the experience far from comfortable, as did the dreadful state of roads at that time. Fuel limitations were also highly restricting – these steam coaches were almost exclusively for carrying upwards of a dozen or more people and, as long as coal was required, the logistics of having a vehicle for individual use were almost impossible. Nonetheless, American inventor Oliver Evans, who had himself created an automatic flour mill before turning his genius to steam travel, predicted that 'the time will come when people will travel in stages moved by steam engines, from one city to another, almost as fast as birds fly, fifteen or twenty miles in an hour'.

It wasn't just primitive technology and transportation practicalities that stymied the early evolution of faster forms of travel. Early nineteenth-century society was not exactly receptive to the notion of creating more rapid, artificially powered, individual speed. Commercial politics inevitably played a part – George Stephenson's Rocket locomotive hit 30 mph way back in 1829, a precursor to mass travel becoming a commodity in the Victorian period. The age of the railways was arriving, and these huge companies were not keen to see any new form of transport offer alternative, bespoke solutions for individual travel. As steam opened up the globe through railways and ships with impressively expansive range and power, vast businesses were investing colossal amounts in establishing a global transport network, and they didn't want to see this lucrative financial future jeopardized. Some turnpikes even made their tolls prohibitively expensive, to deter these steam coaches.

The string of new machines that started to arrive throughout the nineteenth century (some more successful than others) was also the subject of much consternation and concern about the effects on the human body of travelling at higher speeds. One common theory was that a human would suffocate or suffer potentially fatal heart failure and respiratory difficulties if travelling quicker than a horse. This fear

> *One of the most contemptible soul-destroying and devitalising pursuits that the ill-fortune of misguided humanity has ever imposed upon its credulity.*
>
> English philosopher C. E. M. Joad, reacting to the early years of the motor car

had been mooted for some time – back in the eighteenth century, Dr Johnson had rubbished predictions of high-speed travel by stating 'Twenty miles in one hour upon a coach? No man could rush so fast through the air and continue to draw breath!'

The cynics were enraged by accidents such as that in 1834, when Scott Russell's steam coach suffered a collapsed wheel in a street in Paisley, leading to his steam engine exploding. Similar reports of exploding carriages careering around frightened pedestrians were not uncommon, while across in the USA, horrified newspapers detailed how a mother and child had been hit by a similar machine.

*Goldsworth Gurney's steam carriage from 1827. During one trip two years later, 'the fair people of Bath set upon it, burnt their fingers, threw stones, and wounded the poor stoker.'*

Britain was leading the world into the Industrial Age but, ironically, in terms of the developmental modern experience of speed, the heart of the Empire was to lag behind for some time. The nail in the British speed coffin was the passing of the Locomotive Act in 1865, which limited speeds in the countryside to 4 mph (the same as walking) and around towns to just 2 mph. It is commonly quoted that the law stated each vehicle had to be preceded by a man on foot waving a red flag, but a lesser-known condition also required three people to always accompany the vehicle, including not just the flag waver, but also someone to steer and the third person to stoke the boiler. As a direct consequence of this onerous legislation, the development of individual vehicles in Great Britain was suffocated legally for the next thirty years, as well as being completely overshadowed

*Some early champions of the motor car suggested that automobiles would help clean up cities, whose roads were coated in a stinking mass of horse manure.*

by the explosion of railways and further undermined by continuing concerns about health and safety. It's hard to imagine the prejudice and vitriol directed against the early personal transport industry, such as it was, in Britain. There were even sarcastic cartoons in English newspapers mocking the form and function of these prototype vehicles, including one in *The Edinburgh Review* that featured fantastical inventions such as steam walking boots, steam flying machines and even a teapot on wheels. Faced

with such opposition, it is perhaps no surprise that no native-built car of any kind existed in Britain before 1890, meaning Britain was initially lagging somewhat behind much of Europe.

Of course, locomotives already offered speed to the masses, but this was a passive experience, a benign journey with no personal control, albeit one that offered immense liberation (the same would later be true, albeit on a larger scale, of aeroplanes, too). In terms of the adoption of individual speed, as Industrial Britain faltered, continental Europe pushed ahead. Although France would come to pioneer speed and racing in the closing years of the century, it was in Germany where the first, and arguably the biggest, individual breakthrough was made.

*The Benz Motorwagen of 1886, the three-wheeled, tiller-driven pioneer of the modern motor car.*

The history of the internal combustion engine deserves a book of its own and it should be stated that the technology was not necessarily evolved specifically for going quickly. Nonetheless, it was the pioneering work of engineers such as Gustav Otto, Gottlieb Daimler and, ultimately, Karl Benz (along with a varied cast of non-Germanic

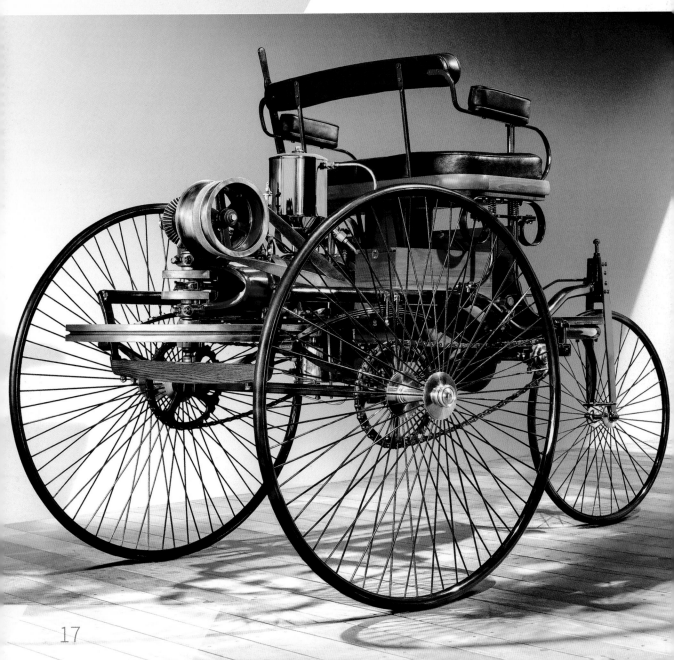

European engineers) that made possible the speed feats contained within this book.

The battle to create the first motor car was fierce and complex, but it is generally acknowledged that the very first such vehicle was the Motorwagen produced by Karl Benz in 1885 and patented the year after. This spindly three-wheeled, tiller-steered car boasted just ⅔ hp, and was powered by a four-stroke, single cylinder internal combustion engine running on coal gas. Famously, it was Benz's wife who would make the world's very first car journey, not the inventor himself. Convinced of her husband's brilliant new invention, but frustrated by his reluctance to test it on public roads, Bertha Benz took the car out one night on a secretive 60-mile trip from Mannheim to her mother's house in Pforzheim. This pioneering journey was fraught with challenges: Bertha had to use a hatpin to clean out a blocked carburetor pipe, a garter to insulate the only electrical ignition cable and even refill with ligroïne (petroleum ether) bought from the shop of a no-doubt bemused chemist. She also stopped off at a shoemaker to get the worn brake pads relined with leather! In so doing, she became the first ever car driver and the first ever car thief, and crucially she set the world's first ever land speed record for a vehicle.

*One of the first Benz catalogues from 1893.*

With his pioneering car suitably test-driven, Karl Benz himself was emboldened to try some adventurous testing of his own. At the time, Germany had a speed limit of 4 mph and, with Benz's machine easily able to double that, the inventor quickly became frustrated. Craftily, Benz invited his local chief of police out for a ride and cleverly arranged for a slow milk float to happen across their path. Initially excited, but then quickly frustrated by the traffic jam, the police chief immediately agreed with Benz that the 4 mph restriction was inappropriate.

As soon as news of the monumental launch of the Benz Motorwagen filtered out across Europe, rival engineering brains started to create their own competing machines - the speed genie was out of the bottle and there was, quite literally, no turning back. With Europe being the undoubted furnace for the early days of motorized speed, a number of propulsion methods immediately vied to power this new phenomenon of the motor car: traditional, very heavy coal-fired engines; volatile gas-powered engines; electricity, which became the market leader for many years; and, bizarrely, some creative speed pioneers even experimented with clockwork propulsion. The experimental efforts were boosted by a crucial shift in public perception towards these new machines and the potential speeds they could achieve. Whereas steam coaches had been stifled and even ridiculed in earlier Victorian society, by the 1890s times were changing. This social context is important: the Long Peace after the Napoleonic Wars had been complemented by the aforementioned establishment of the railways as a settled, relatively safe and efficient way to travel long distances. By the late nineteenth century, the blossoming of modern cities and, with that, a more widespread affluence meant that the upper reaches of Western society were becoming increasingly open to new, more personal (albeit expensive) ways to travel.

Soon, the engineering brains of Europe were creating a number of early cars, all vying for the attention and wallets of the wealthy elite. It must be noted that these very early machines were not exactly designed for speed. In fact, so unreliable were many of the first motor cars that going fast was always a secondary ambition to simply going at all. For a while, car owners often had servants follow them on horseback, in case their mechanical ride faltered (again), somewhat defeating the object of this new method of transport. However, over time, a generation of brilliant engineers was able to increasingly inject reliability into their machines, meaning their inquisitive minds could start to turn to other matters, such as generating more speed. Moreover, once the public had started buying these vehicles - by 1901, Benz had sold 2300 - the idea of going quicker had started to ferment in the consciousness of the wider population, not just society's elite. Therein lay the genesis of one of the modern world's most formative and central impulses: the notion of going more rapidly, not just to get to a destination more quickly ... but *to be faster than everyone else.*

# Chapter 2

# The Birth of the Motor Race and
# Land Speed Record

*When speed gets in the blood, one must drive to live.*

German racing driver Rudolf Caracciola

The early days of the motor car were spent in the pursuit of reliability rather than speed, and as such the first races were in fact endurance trials. The general consensus of automotive sources suggests that the first ever motor race was on 22 July 1894, when the Parisian magazine *Le Petit Journal* organized an event to run from the French capital to Rouen. This was very much a test of endurance – the competitors even stopped for lunch at Mantes-la-Jolie, where they chatted with spectators and locals – but it is the use of the word 'race' in the reporting of the day that seems to have secured this occasion's status as the first ever such event.

Given the pioneering nature of this moment, one might suspect a scarcity of entrants, but in fact 102 competitors paid the 10 franc fee to enter; sixty-nine cars attempted the 31-mile selection event, and these were then whittled down to the final twenty-five serious competitors who made it to the start line of the main 79-mile race. First past the post was the notorious duellist Count Jules-Albert de Dion in his eponymous car, but vehicles made by Panhard et Levassor and Peugeot were selected for awards to acknowledge their speed, handling characteristics and safety attributes.

The top cars managed to average around 12 mph. Interestingly, by way of reflecting that certain elements of society were still divided over the appeal of going quickly, *Le Petit Journal* later withdrew its backing for any future such events, expressing concerns about its readership's perception of encouraging excessive speed.

*Early motoring journals did not always enjoy great support: Le Petit Journal championed, then later withdrew its support for, racing due to concerns about its readers' disapproval. In Britain, Autocar launched in 1895 only to be met by this less than kind review in The Sketch: 'It is published in the interests of the mechanically propelled road carriage. What next?!'*

# Le Petit Journal

### SUPPLÉMENT ILLUSTRÉ

**TOUS LES JOURS**
Le Petit Journal
5 Centimes

Huit pages : CINQ centimes

**TOUS LES DIMANCHES**
Le Supplément illustré
5 Centimes

Cinquième année     LUNDI 6 AOUT 1894     Numéro 194

Concours du « Petit Journal »

## LES VOITURES SANS CHEVAUX

The Lohner-Porsche Mixed Hybrid electric car of the late 1890s. By this point, speed was becoming more commonplace, leading to the very first speeding tickets, such as one at 8 mph given to a racer called Walter Arnold, who was apparently chased by a policeman on a bicycle for travelling at the heady speed in a 2 mph zone. Mr Arnold was defended by a Mr Cripps who, according to the court report in the London Daily News on 30 January 1896, argued that the law should not apply to the new transport of horseless carriages. His ingenious defence didn't work – Arnold was fined a shilling for his recklessness. (Fast-forwarding to 2003, an American man was caught speeding in his hypercar allegedly at 242 mph in a 75 mph zone.)

While Germany had led the way with early engine design, many of the earliest motor car races were centred around Paris. French manufacturers were pre-eminent in both automobile manufacture and racing and, unlike *Le Petit Journal,* as a general rule the native French media enthusiastically supported such events. Perhaps not surprisingly, many of these formative races were beset with problems, accidents, injuries and even collisions with cattle!

At this point, the quickest early cars were very often electric. In the USA, the Electric Carriage and Wagon Company of Philadelphia ran a fleet of electric taxis in New York in the 1890s. Further, despite the huge weight of their elementary batteries, the immediate torque and simplicity of electric power also proved very popular with a new breed of racer that was emerging – the very first land speed pioneers.

The decade after Benz's 1885 Motorwagen had seen the engineering impetus behind motor cars fragment, with the majority pursuing reliability while a smaller, but nonetheless sizeable, element began to prioritize speed above all else. This was an important moment of distinction in the history of speed, mechanically propelled machines now being perceived as a means of creating pure speed (previously unheard-of speed, in fact), rather than merely engineering a reliable new method of transport. As already noted, going fast – or faster than the next person – is certainly a basic human instinct, but add to that base impulse the excitement and draw of new technology, and with it the accompanying glamour and social admiration, then it is easy to see why, once reliability and decent endurance were an engineering staple, the speed-freaks came out to play. And there are no more remarkable early speed merchants than two charismatic rivals, the Frenchman Comte de Chasseloup-Laubat and his arch-nemesis, the Belgian Camille Jenatzy, otherwise known as the Red Devil, so called because of his flaming red beard and hair.

On a cold and wet 18 December 1898, the Comte de Chasseloup-Laubat climbed on top of his electric car, known as the Jeantaud, on a road in Achères near Paris. Powered by heavy lead-acid Fulman batteries, the Jeantaud had the first-ever use of a steering wheel, which quickly became the preferred option compared to the previously commonplace, but hardly easy-to-use, tiller.

The stage was set on a timed 2-kilometre flat road, with the car travelling in one direction only. The first half of the run was intended for standing start times, the second half for flying start records, both of which were overseen by no less than six timekeepers. The dusty road was pocked with ruts and loose gravel, and there were no safety barriers or driver protection. Safety was almost non-existent, with the Comte perched precariously on top of the low, boat-shaped vehicle, with only his legs actually inside the car. He wore a basic leather skullcap helmet, as his huge, heavy and hard-to-control beast of a car thundered along the uneven road, teetering on painfully thin and unreliable pneumatic tyres.

Using the car's 36 hp to its full capacity, the Jeantaud ran for just 57 seconds over a flying kilometre, reaching 39.24 mph and in doing so setting the first universally recognized world land speed record. As the Comte rushed past the dozens of bewildered spectators, fellow early racers and marshals, his car was said to be 'trailing a few blue sparks and [have] a slight tang of ozone'. Notably, at that point in time the speed record for a push bike across a flying kilometre was actually slightly quicker!

Across in Belgium, the fierce patriot Red Devil Jenatzy was perturbed by the idea of a Frenchman being the fastest person on earth. Jenatzy had been the only notable absence near Paris when the Comte set the first ever speed record, and the two rivals would go head to head several times over the coming months and years. These remarkable early days of brutal speed chasing saw international competition become a constant feature of speed records, as rival individuals battled to secure the crown not just for themselves but also for their country.

As a child, Jenatzy had competed in bicycle races but constantly craved greater speed and so threw himself into the world of electromechanical engineering, designing electric vehicles and numerous early hybrid systems. He even won a renowned hill climb in a self-built electric dog cart, and soon after started competing in speed trials. Thus he came to battle with the Comte, in a rivalry that is the stuff of legend in speed circles. Time and again these two opponents would fight against each other for the top speed mark, sitting atop immensely dangerous cars that were attempting to reach speeds no human had ever previously achieved, with no apparent fear of their seemingly imminent death. All that mattered was being quicker than their rival. Most famous of all these trials was the notorious speed duel between these two on 17 January 1899, using a civilian road just west of Paris, prompted by Jenatzy actually penning a letter to the Comte, challenging him in person.

*Camille Jenatzy – the Red Devil – the first person to reach over 60 mph and one of the greatest mavericks in the history of speed.*

28

The Association Générale de l'Automobile in Paris (later known as the Fédération Internationale de l'Automobile, FIA) took it upon itself to be the overseer of many aspects of motorsport, including speed record runs. Over a decade after Jenatzy set his records, they later decreed that in future a record would only be acknowledged if two runs were made, in opposite directions and within an hour of each other, in order to take into account the benefits of gradient and wind.

Determined to emerge as the ultimate victor against his French adversary, Jenatzy designed a 4-metre long, cigar-shaped, tiller-steered electric vehicle by the name of *Jamais Contente*, using a pair of 25-kilowatt electric motors fed by batteries delivering approximately 68 hp. The car was part-built in partinium, a light alloy combining aluminium, tungsten and magnesium. Jenatzy's logical and scientific brain was paired with an unquenchable thirst for speed, and he was often quoted as saying, 'Nothing is as exciting as racing'. Clearly his wife was not so taken; '*Jamais Contente*' translates as 'Never Content', which some sources suggest was a nod to his partner's dissatisfaction at his constant travelling to, and competing in, international speed competitions.

On the mid-January 1899 day of the duel, Jenatzy fired the first shot, hitting 41.42 mph, breaking the speed record on his first attempt; the Comte duly responded with 43.69 mph, burning out the motor of his Jeantaud just 200 metres from the finish in the process! This classic speed battle was followed by a sequence of rival record attempts by the two arch-enemies over the coming weeks, which saw the top speed jump up to 57.6 mph by the start of the next month, a significant percentage increment. In so doing, and with no sign of these two speed obsessives stepping back from battle, the Automobile Club de France became involved, leading to many of the early regulations and rules for land speed record attempts being hastily put in place.

Both men were constantly updating their cars. Jenatzy created an engine using secondary coils that was capable of revving at 900 rpm, considered quite remarkable at the time. Yet another challenge was issued for 1 April, but a mix-up meant that Jenatzy's run was not timed correctly. Returning to the same road near Paris at the end of the month, this time accompanied by ever-growing crowds of fascinated spectators (dangerously) lining the course, Jenatzy completed a solo run timed at 65.79 mph. That equates to comfortably more than a mile a minute, making him the first person to ever drive at more than 100km/h. This was a record that would stand for three years. The speed mark achieved by this pivotal twin electric motor vehicle led to the notion of 0-60 mph becoming a staple measure of how fast a car is able to accelerate.

The Red Devil would ultimately break the land speed record three times before hanging up his racing gloves for good. Reflecting on what it felt like to travel at a speed that contemporary science originally believed was too quick for the human body to survive, Jenatzy said: 'The car in which you travel seems to leave the ground and hurl itself forward like a projectile ricocheting along the ground.'

Jenatzy had once prophesied that he would die in a Mercedes. He was understandably drawn to the likes of that German marque's 50 mph Simplex 35 bhp as the forefather of the fast car. The Simplex is considered by many to be the first ever supercar, not least because early aeroplanes would not travel this fast for another ten years. However, the Grim Reaper caught up with the speeding Devil in somewhat less velocious circumstances. Out hunting with his pals in Africa, Jenatzy hid behind a bush and made animal noises to startle his co-hunters for merriment - suitably alarmed, they promptly shot him. He made his final automotive dash on the way to hospital but ran out of time, bleeding to death on the back seat ... of a Mercedes.

# Chapter 3

# The Speed Kings Gather

*To rush through the air at the speed of a torpedo boat destroyer, down a narrow, curving road enclosed with hedges and without being able to see what was in front of us, was a novel and thrilling experience.*

Reporter for *The Automotor Journal*, writing about his experience as a passenger on the London to Brighton race of 1896

While Germany had made the breakthrough and 1890s France proved to be a hotbed of automobile innovation, across in Britain it wasn't until 1896 that the debilitating Locomotive Act was repealed - this apparent moment of motoring liberation wasn't exactly a mandate for land speed records, but the newly set limit of 14 mph did at least mean the previously stillborn British car industry could at last get off the ground. The instant and rabid interest that quickly followed this repeal seems to suggest that there was a significant pent-up British demand for this new chance to go fast.

Within a few years, Britain became fully immersed in the new science of speed, as demonstrated by the first ever motor car run from London to Brighton in 1896, including a ceremonial tearing up of a red flag at the start line (the annual London-Brighton race is now the oldest surviving motoring event in the world). Similar events in Europe and also across the Atlantic (such as the Gordon Bennett Cup) would quickly grow in

*Cars being tested at Crystal Palace in 1902.*

popularity, although it should be noted that many of these events were still essentially endurance races.

Inevitably, as safety was almost non-existent, with these early cars hitting ever quicker speeds with little thought for the consequences of a crash, there were many terrible accidents. The science of automotive speed was effectively being made up as each year went by, so it was no surprise that the first fatality of a pedestrian came in 1896, when a Mrs Bridget Driscol was hit and killed by a car while crossing the street in Crystal Palace, south London. The first British fatality of a car driver was recorded in February 1898, when Henry Lindfield of Brighton died from shock the day after losing a leg underneath his overturned car. This first car death was attributed in the press to excessive speed. Unhelpful media hysteria occasionally fuelled the remaining pockets of paranoia, but the scaremongering

reports about early car crashes and fatalities was disproportionate to the facts – in France in 1900, 150 people were killed by horses and trams in Paris, but only 2 by cars, the same number as by bicycles.

Despite these remaining doubters, by the end of the nineteenth century public cynicism towards speed had begun to morph into fascination. By the first years of the new century, gone were the fears and doubts of the previous decades; instead,

enthusiastic crowds flocked to any motor car race that was staged. One example was the Southport Speed Trials, as this extract from the 5 October 1903 edition of the *Manchester Courier and Lancashire General Advertiser* shows:

*No local [event] has attracted such enormous crowds as the motor speed trials which were successfully concluded today. The weather in the morning was wet and cheerless; but, despite this, at an early hour heavily laden*

*Brooklands became an early and world-famous hub of speed obsessives and racers after its 1907 opening.*

*trains arrived from all quarters ... the barriers along the whole length of the promenade track were thickly lined by spectators ... by half-past two it was estimated that 50,000 spectators were present. The grandstands erected in front of the hotels and principal houses were packed with fashionably dressed ladies and gentlemen whilst behind the stout barriers along the roadside, thousands of men, women and children struggled to catch a glimpse of the competitors as they flew past on their machines.*

By this point in the story, the allure of speed was simply proving too enticing to be ignored. In 1902, the (later Royal) Automobile Club of Great Britain organized what is considered by many to be the first race on British soil, at Bexhill-on-Sea, attracting thousands of spectators. As it became apparent that city and public road racing was inherently very dangerous for all concerned, purpose-built circuits began to spring up. At huge personal cost, British entrepreneur Hugh F. Locke King created Brooklands in 1907, the world's first purpose-built racing circuit, in the grounds of his estate, measuring 2.75 miles long, 100 feet wide and manufactured from concrete, complete with two long straights and 30-foot-high banked curves. The endeavour almost bankrupted him. The circuit did, nonetheless, allow the British contingent of early race drivers and speed merchants such as Selwyn Francis Edge, George E. Stanley and L. G.

This 1906 brochure was aimed at early petrolheads – initially christened 'Autocarists'.

Hornsted to respond to their European rivals more frequently. Across in the USA, the first purpose-built race track was created by motoring entrepreneur Carl G. Fisher at the Indianapolis Motor Speedway in 1909. The international speed stakes were entering a new adversarial era.

To be a land speed record holder (then, and now) is to know that there is always someone else waiting in the wings to snatch away the title. Jenatzy and the Comte (who died aged just 36) had barely turned their engines off when Frenchman Léon Serpollet took his fantastically named Œuf de Pâques

*One of 'the most amusing sights the track can offer is to watch anybody attempting to climb the banking on foot. They start so boldly, and usually finish by turning hurriedly round and slithering down again ... I should say it would be practically impossible for anybody to climb the banking at its steepest point unless equipped with rubber soles, and even then it would be no easy task.'*
*Extract from* Motorsport *magazine about Brooklands.*

(Easter Egg) ovoid steam car to 75.06 mph in 1902. This was helped in part by his unique flash boiler system, which made steam a much more usable source of power for automobiles. In newspaper interviews afterwards, Serpollet acknowledged that the naysayers predicting certain death if human bodies were put through such speeds had been on his mind, admitting that he had held his breath for the entire 30-second run and had eventually turned his head to the side to inhale.

In these very early days of the pursuit of being the fastest on earth, more speed required more power, as early aerodynamics was primitive and, at times, completely self-

defeating. A classic example of this brutish approach was when mass-market automotive pioneer Henry Ford joined the fray, aiming to promote his new cars to the public at the New York Motor Show. The car he used had actually previously been wrecked during a race, claiming the life of the driver, but Ford rebuilt it, this time with a colossal power plant named after the famous Arrow train, which boasted a frankly bizarre capacity of 16,708 cc. In 1904, Ford would actually surpass the world speed record on an ice track carved into the bay around the frozen Lake St Clair in Michigan by hitting 91.37 mph in this inline four-cylinder, 72 hp car. But, unlike many of his peers in the speed world, Ford later said that he had been so frightened by

*Above: Increasingly reliable tyres towards the end of the 1890s and into the first decade of the new century enabled speeds to increase swiftly.*

the experience that he would never get into a racing car again. Worse still, his efforts were not officially ratified, as the French ACF had not sanctioned the timing equipment.

As the century advanced, electric cars would become too expensive and heavy to keep up with rival propulsion methods. Steam was considered too unreliable, cumbersome and range-limited – but the previously third-placed petrol engine was growing more and more advanced, reliable, cheaper to run and, with a network of petrol stations being established, increasingly the power mode of choice for road-going cars. This was also mirrored in the world of extreme speed. First, Baron Pierre de Caters' petrol-powered

car matched the Easter Egg's record, and then in August 1902 a vehicle driven by an American millionaire, William K. Vanderbilt, became the first petrol car to claim the land speed record, hitting 76.03 mph, again in France. Thereafter, there was a glut of record attempts in quick succession, such as that of Louis Rigolly, who became the first man to hit 100 mph in July 1904 in his Gobron-Brillié on a 1-kilometre beach course near Ostend.

Exceptions such as the understandably cautious Ford aside, a peculiar breed of racers was starting to emerge who were willing to literally risk everything to be able to say they had driven faster than any human before them. It is hard to overstate how much these

early speed pioneers really were putting themselves at immense, potentially fatal, risk. Although much faster land speed cars of later years would also risk danger due to the massive speeds attained, by then the safety precautions would have evolved to the point of being state of the art. But, back in the first decade of the new century, these early pioneers apparently had no fear of dying at any moment. Safety? Wear a well-made leather cap. Barriers? Too expensive. Aerodynamics? Simply bend forward over the steering wheel. As well as the aforementioned racers, other courageous and possibly foolhardy men such as Arthur Duray, Henri Fournier and Maurice Augières are just a few more examples of the brave souls who pushed and pushed to be the fastest. Land speed historian Lynn Hughes has likened these individuals to the astronauts who landed on the moon, given that they simply did not know at the time what would happen to the human body at these unprecedented speeds, in an environment that no human had ever experienced before.

Perhaps one of the most dangerous speed runs of this perilous early period was that of the Stanley brothers' steam-powered Rocket in Daytona Beach, for the Speed Week in 1906. According to land speed expert Don Wales in his book *Land Speed Records*, the red car looked like 'an upturned canoe' and the chosen venue of Daytona Beach suffered from sands that were not in the best condition. Undeterred, the Stanley brothers chose to put their maintenance man, Fred Marriott, in the driver's seat and, despite his relative lack of racing experience, their man rewarded them with a record speed of 127.6 mph.

The Stanley brothers were not finished yet – fearing a tide of public opinion moving against their beloved steam power and towards the internal combustion engine, the following year they created an absolute monster of a car, weighing 1600 lbs, with the steam pressure cranked up to a massive 1300 psi. This time Fred took a 9-mile run-up and was reported to have hit the flying start already travelling at 198 mph.

Unfortunately, during one run at around 140 mph, Fred's huge car hit a bevelled gully hiding in the shining sands, which launched the Rocket into the sky, turning it onto its side while still airborne, after which it smashed into the ground and cartwheeled 100 feet along the beach, showering the entire scene with shrapnel and debris.

Remarkably, when marshals ran over to the mangled wreckage, they found maintenance man Fred still alive. He'd suffered four cracked ribs, a broken breastbone and facial lacerations, and when he turned over they saw that his right eye was hanging out of its socket. A bystander who happened to be a Mexican doctor on holiday there escorted Fred to a nearby hotel and gently slid his eyeball back into its socket with a sugar spoon, at which point Fred was reported to have smiled and said: 'Thanks Doc! Now it's the best eye I have!'

*Opposite and below: In the first decades, motor cars were very expensive, way beyond the means of the average person. Therefore, the speed they offered was out of reach for the majority.*

# Chapter 4

# Speed as a
# Pheremone

*I myself have never travelled at much more than eighty miles an hour in a car; but those who drunk a stronger beverage of this strange intoxicant tell me that new marvels await anyone who has the opportunity of passing the hundred mark... two hundred miles an hour must be absolute torture!*

Author and philosopher Aldous Huxley

When did speed become glamorous? Certainly at the dawn of modern transport, speed was perceived as beneficial and desirable. This recognized advantage soon transformed into something more attractive as - rightly or wrongly - speed became inextricably associated with glamour.

The earliest motor cars were very much the domain of the wealthy. When Benz's Motorwagen was first sold in the late 1880s, the revolutionary machine cost 3000 German marks, at a time when most people were only earning hundreds of marks per year. Early automobiles were often custom-built, with expensive coachwork bespoke to each customer. The first generation of land speed and racing drivers were invariably wealthy and charismatic individuals, sprinkling further doses of glamour on the formative years of speed. Both road-going cars and land speed vehicles were simply unattainable to the wider population, so in those people any speed thrill at this point was entirely vicarious - a cultural distance that may itself have strengthened the attraction.

That said, there is evidence that in certain quarters of the twentieth century speed remained a social pariah. Some American car owners reported being stoned by unimpressed crowds whenever they drove through working-class neighbourhoods. This interclass envy would be so great that a few years later President Woodrow Wilson would declare the automobile to be 'the greatest incitement of the poor to socialism'. For a long time, access to mechanized speed was confined by money, stature, gender and proximity to automobile production, all factors restricting who might or might not be able to travel at speed.

Of course, the advent of cheap mass production cars by the likes of Henry Ford et al around 1908 changed the demography of car ownership. Although these mass market vehicles were not racing cars, to own one at a time when personal travel was otherwise restricted to public transport or walking would have certainly injected a new level of speed into the general public's experience, albeit at a relatively modest velocity. In many ways, the mass-produced car represented a belated personification of all the engineering developments of the Industrial Revolution, neatly captured in millions of mechanical, personal mobility revolutions – in 1907, there were 62,000 cars made globally but by 1913 that figure had risen nearly tenfold, to over 606,000. Although these cars were not particularly fast, that is a relative statement; they certainly were if the alternative was walking or using a horse. Crucially, as Enda Duffy theorizes in his brilliant work, *The Speed Handbook*, cars made the experience of speed active, rather than passive, which in turn personalized the process. Indeed, so important is the car to the modern world that Duffy calls this machine 'a modernist mobile architecture'.

*A typical gathering of so-called 'Gentlemen Racers' competing after the First World War. Across in the USA, one such racing legend, land speed competitor and racer Ralph DePalma, crashed during a road race and was impaled on a corn stalk; it took him eleven weeks to recover well enough to leave hospital. DePalma has one of the greatest win rates of any speed merchant, having secured the chequered flag in 2557 out of the 2889 races he entered.*

Sadly, any growing sense of speed becoming a part of everyday twentieth-century life came to a crashing and brutal halt with the outbreak of the First World War. Engineering during the war years saw many significant advances, although these were initially designed for use in conflict, not on public roads. The Great War and immediately ensuing austere recovery years necessarily shunned expensive cars and, by association, speed as an indulgence was widely frowned upon. The shell-shocked car world looked for economy, utility and affordability. An initial post-war lack of raw materials further diluted any commercial interest in speed.

However, the human interest in speed has a habit of resurfacing; it seems the impulse can be postponed but never cancelled. The land speed pioneers of this era attracted much attention (as will be detailed in the next chapter), but away from the beaches and sands of these ultra-high speed fanatics, by the 1920s the West was beginning to resurface after the horrors of war, and subsequently a golden period of mass-market speed was just around the corner.

By this point, a large number of people owned cars thanks to a booming global economy and the birth of consumer credit; this was truly the age of the mass-produced car - nearly a million Model Ts were sold in 1920 alone. Inadvertently this exacerbated the glamorization of speed because the growth of car ownership persuaded wealthier people to separate themselves from these cheap vehicles by acquiring more and more expensive cars. Some did this with ultra-luxury makes such as Rolls-Royce and Duesenburg; the latter were considered the height of extravagance in the USA - the chassis alone cost nineteen times more than a $400 Ford Model T. Others chose to separate themselves using speed - which always costs money, too. During this period, speed became inextricably linked with class.

Also in the 1920s, a glut of road cars was available that were capable of very high speeds: despite being later than the Simplex, the significantly more powerful and stylish Mercedes SSK is regarded by some as the world's first supercar, while the Bugatti Type 57, Stutz Bearcat and Alfa Romeo 8C Tipo B Monoposto were all beautifully engineered and extremely quick. Again, these were way beyond the average person's means, but the very fact that some of these were ostensibly road cars that could also (in certain instances) win on the race track began a period that would indelibly secure speed and glamour as inextricable bedfellows. Enter the world of the Gentleman Racer ...

The backdrop to this enticing chapter in the history of speed is the Roaring Twenties, a period when elements of Western society obsessed over extravagance, progress and indulgence. It was a decade where fast money, fast living, fast communications and fast cars created a veneer of aspiration and success in a world that, so it transpired, was actually hurtling towards the jaws of the Great Depression. Air travel was beginning to take shape as a potentially new and exciting industry of the future, while industrial and financial growth in many countries enjoyed a focus on a newly burgeoning consumer economy. Art Deco, jazz, the Charleston, the talkies at cinemas, the growing use of telephones and radio, new electrical appliances in homes such as fridges, vacuums and washing machines ... in every corner of Western society the pace of life was rapidly increasing. Expressionism and Surrealism in the art world, and seminal novels such as *The Great Gatsby* reinforced the sense that modernity was paramount. This was also the first modern era that fawned over the cult of celebrity - movie stars such as Charlie Chaplin, Douglas Fairbanks, Harold Lloyd, Buster Keaton, sports heroes (baseball stars Babe Ruth, boxer Jack Dempsey and swimmer/actor Johnny Weissmuller) and other famous faces such as aviator Charles Lindbergh preoccupied the world with a fanaticism not seen before. Votes for women and progressive liberalism flourished, and encouraged previously oppressed areas of society. Not without justification do the French call this period *les années folles*, or the crazy years.

The importance of speed in 1920s society can be highlighted by the Futurist movement, which originated in Italy in the early twentieth century. Its members' obsession was modernity - speed, new technology, industry, youth, inventions such as the car and aeroplane ... essentially a celebration of

*Established by Frederick Simms in 1897 as the Automobile Club of Great Britain and Ireland, the club is the oldest motoring institution in the United Kingdom and the second oldest in the world.*

modernity and progress. The founder of this movement, Filippo Tommaso Marinetti, stated in 1909: 'The world's magnificence has been enriched by a new beauty: the beauty of speed.' The movement was complex, becoming imbibed with avant-garde art such as Cubism - and seemingly promoting violence, too, as well as some apparent advocacy of fascism. Despite this, Futurism enjoyed some international popularity in countries such as Russia, Britain and Belgium. Although the movement effectively died out when its founder Marinetti passed away in 1944, the central tenets of celebrating modernity, speed, youth, technology and so on remain ever present in Western society and are relevant to this study.

# Chapter 5

# The Bentley Boys and the Bugatti Queen

*My nervousness before the start was proportionately great, but at last we were off, down the street towards Pontlieue, with the three Bentleys almost arm in arm at the head of a long procession. It was plain from the start then, that the race was going to be run at a very great speed ... the thought gave me the greatest pleasure.*

Sir Tim Birkin, writing about his 1928 Le Mans in his book, *Full Throttle*

In the world of speed, the history books usually depict the Roaring Twenties as a time of dashing Gentlemen Racers and high-speed, high-society playboys, soaking in the admiring glances of countless beautiful women. The epitome of this notion were the Bentley Boys, an ultra-wealthy jet set of mavericks and adventurers who drove hard and partied even harder – among their numbers were a pearl fisherman, a diamond magnate and various high-profile financiers. Suave and dashing mavericks such as Woolf Barnato, who had a mock-Tudor pub built in the basement of his mansion, seemed straight out of the movies rather than being a real-life racing driver. And at the centre of this seductive glamour and global fame were their incredible Bentley racing cars – a variety of huge, sublimely engineered machines capable of being driven leisurely to a track, whereupon the headlights would be removed and luggage taken out, ready for a string of courageous drivers to hammer their beasts around the circuit. Afterwards, to

the admiring glances of many, these drivers would retire to the garages and pits to smoke cigars, drink fine whiskies and soak in the smell of oil, petrol and society's admiration, before reattaching their headlights and roaring off home to their country mansions. This wasn't all show – throughout the twenties, the Bentley Boys scooped multiple race wins, broke many track records and effectively dominated the world's most prestigious endurance event at Le Mans.

In terms of raw speed, there is one Bentley from this period that symbolizes the priorities of this clique: the infamous Blower. With aerodynamics still in its relative infancy, there was still a belief that more power equated to more speed. Bentley Motors were aware that their continental rivals were starting to catch up on the track and so, in their attempts to stay ahead of the game, they created the huge 6.5-litre Speed Six, which won many races but was derided by rival French manufacturer Ettore Bugatti as 'the world's fastest lorry'. However, for road cars, simply cramming a bigger and ever mightier engine under the bonnet had limitations of scale and practicality, so the engineers looked at other ways to make their machines more powerful and therefore speedier. Under the tutelage of former fighter pilot Sir Henry 'Tim' Birkin and against the express wishes of founder W. O. Bentley himself, engineer Amherst Villiers took a 4.5-litre Bentley and strapped an enormous supercharger in front of the radiator. This powerful engineering addition was essentially an air pump that forced more oxygen into the cylinders of the engine, creating a bigger internal explosion and therefore more power. The earliest superchargers had surfaced almost a century earlier, and many were initially used to stoke blast furnaces. With the Blower, siting the supercharger between the engine and the carburetors - simply, beautifully, leaving it exposed between the two front wheels for all to see - was an unashamedly proud statement of its *raison d'être*: speed.

The Blower Bentley, proudly sporting its supercharger front and centre of the car, in its unashamed quest for more speed.

Birkin's endeavour was championed and indeed sponsored by an eccentric race horse owner called Dorothy Wyndham Paget, who in later life lived nocturnally, eating breakfast at 6:30 p.m. and lunch at 10 p.m. She was an accomplished racer herself and, after taking lessons from Birkin, decided to underwrite the development costs of the Blower.

The supercharging trick created a massive power boost of almost 60 per cent compared to the non-supercharged 4.5-litre Bentley touring equivalent (in race trim, the engine now produced 240 hp). The Blower won a number of races (albeit lower-profile ones) and was by no means the most winning Bentley, dogged as it was by reliability issues. That said, one example did set a record speed of 137.96 mph at Brooklands in March 1932, with reports suggesting that, due to the uneven concrete surface of the Surrey race track, the car spent much of the lap airborne.

What the Blower Bentley supremely represents is the most blatant display of the 'more is better' ethos that so neatly reflected society in the 1920s, and the place of speed in the lexicon of the period. With only fifty-five Blowers ever made, and taking into account the car's significance in the history of speed, it is little wonder that prime examples are among some of the most collectible and valuable cars in the world. Sadly, neither the Blower nor Birkin would live much past the end of the Roaring Twenties. Bentley withdrew from racing in 1930, and although Birkin enjoyed some high-profile success –

*Above and opposite: Gentlemen Racers came from the super-wealthy upper echelons of high society and played a significant role in the glamorisation of speed.*

including winning Le Mans in an Alfa Romeo – he later burnt his arm on a hot exhaust pipe while picking up a cigarette lighter during a pit stop at the Tripoli Grand Prix. Then a possible combination of this infected wound and malaria took his life in June 1933; he was just thirty-six.

In the 1920s and 1930s, the birth of the more affordable sports car allowed those with relatively modest incomes to experience greater personal speed. While the vast majority of car owners were still unable to buy high-speed vehicles, a number of early, diminutive sports cars in the 1930s did extend the enjoyment beyond the upper classes. Numerous cars such as MG, Alvis, the Morgan three-wheelers, Fiat's Ballila 508S and the BSA Scout serviced what would prove to be a growing market for cars that were quicker than an everyday machine but not so expensive as to be beyond the reach of all but the richest of thrill-seekers. Although these cars may not have offered Bentley Blower speeds, they did open up the idea of a car for the wider public that was capable of decent speed, a notion that motor manufacturers would forever continue to exploit with great success.

The era of the Gentleman Racer was without doubt a golden period for speed. The accepted mythology reinforces the male dominance of these kings of speed, with little room for those from a lower class – or, indeed, women. However, scratch a little deeper into this apparently male world of speed pursuits and it is not hard to find women who were also pushing the boundaries, perhaps none more so than Hellé Nice, otherwise known as the

Queen of Speed and the Bugatti Queen. Her early career had been an altogether different version of 'racy' – posing for saucy photographs, working as an artist's nude muse, and dancing in cabaret and music hall establishments all around Europe, including many of dubious character. According to accounts of the day, her striking blue eyes enthralled many of the male suitors who watched and adored her, and would later play a pivotal part in her frankly astonishing racing career.

In 1929, while on a skiing holiday, Nice was caught up in an avalanche and damaged her knee so badly that her dancing career was terminated overnight. Instead of wallowing in self-pity, she decided this was the chance to finally pursue her childhood dream: to race cars. Back in

*The lithe and sinuous 1935 Bugatti Aérolithe concept car, a precursor to the iconic Type 57SC, of which only four were made and, at the time of writing, are said to be valued at around £114 million each.*

1903, as a 3-year-old holding hands with her schoolteacher, she had seen the Paris-Madrid race roar through her village in south-western Paris, and had been utterly captivated by the noisy, smelly and, above all, super-fast machines that were hurtling past. As a young woman, as soon as she'd saved enough money from her dancing, she had bought a small Citroën and spent much of the 1920s driving spiritedly around France and Europe, albeit never once in a competition or race. In fact, several applications for her to race were turned down because of her gender.

On one of these trips, she'd become acquainted with the wealthy owner of a car parts business. Fast-forward to 1929, and the same businessman was now looking for an opportunity to promote his company, which was suffering from the effects of the Great Depression. Together, he and Nice cooked up the idea to enter her into the 1929 all-women's grand prix at Montlhéry.

*During the Sao Paolo Grand Prix, Nice swerved to avoid reckless spectators, resulting in a horrific crash that killed six and left her severely injured.*

According to some sources, Nice prepared for the race the night before by indulging in 'a long night of champagne, morphine and sex'. Despite this, and being a complete unknown undertaking her first race against some of the era's finest female drivers, the inspiring and clearly naturally gifted Nice took her Omega-Six to victory, smashing the female land speed record in the process. 'The driving was magnificent,' hailed the newspaper *L'Intransigeant*. 'Nobody who saw it would feel able to argue that women drive less well than men.'

Her astounding debut victory drew the attention of Ettore Bugatti, the enigmatic entrepreneur who headed up the legendary French car marque. Looking for a new driver for his race team, Bugatti contacted Nice the very next day and pronounced that her startlingly blue eyes were 'the perfect match for the colour of my Bugattis'. However unusual the reasons for her recruitment, Nice proved to be a cunning and brave driver, sweeping to multiple victories for her new French team. She would remain the only female on the Grand Prix circuit for several years to come.

Away from the circuits of Europe, Nice partied as hard as the high-society men she was perennially surrounded by, but she was no rich man's plaything – her racing reputation was fierce, she was renowned for never giving up and she opined to anyone who would listen about the thrill of having a 'great roaring race car in my hands that wants only to go faster'. She frequently raced in exhibitions with no helmet, telling people that 'the crowds always like to see my hair when I am driving'.

Consistent with the inherently dangerous nature of early motorsport, in 1936 Nice suffered a horrific accident in her Alfa Romeo at the Brazilian Grand Prix that left six people dead and Nice in a coma for days – when race marshals arrived at the scene of the crash, she was so badly injured and apparently lifeless that initially her motionless body was laid out alongside the dead; recuperation was slow, her memory never fully recovered and observers suggested that her lightning-quick speed was forever blunted. She won her last race just a month before the Second World War started; during the conflict, all racing activity was necessarily halted just at a time when Nice might have been able to recover to her peak. By the time the war was over, she was increasingly troubled by memory loss, and her reputation was sullied by an unsubstantiated accusation of Nazi sympathizing. The Queen of Speed fell into destitution and isolation, at one point relying on donations from an actors' charity. Her biographer, Miranda Seymour, quotes neighbours seeing Nice 'taking the milk out of the cats' saucers because she had nothing to eat or drink'. The Bugatti Queen, Hellé Nice, died in abject poverty in a tiny attic bedsit in southern France in 1984.

*'It's all I ever ask for, just to show what I can do without a handicap against men.'* Hellé Nice speaking in 1930.

# Chapter 6

# The Age of Monsters

*No one will deny that the joys of sheer speed possess an extraordinary fascination but, before taking the wheel of the Sunbeam, I had no idea of the wonderful sensation of driving at a really high velocity. One only has to sit behind the big engine and let the car go on a good stretch of sand to feel as if some supernatural force were at work; a force, which though controlled by the hand of man, is so terrific as to inspire awe. Every run I take on the big car makes me feel ten years younger.*

Sir Malcolm Campbell

While Henry Ford and his ilk were making millions from motoring for the masses, the speed merchants never stopped pursuing their peculiarly niche obsession. If Britain had initially lagged behind in the early days of automotive development - and, by association, land speed - in the 1920s the country thrust itself very much to the forefront of this new race to produce the fastest machine on earth. The two kingpins of this first Great British speed era were Sir Malcolm Campbell and Sir Henry Segrave, both former soldiers, but two very different characters. Fiercely patriotic, these speed rivals shared an obsession to ensure the fastest person in the world was a Brit. The tales of their land speed record attempts and the machines they drove are the exploits of speed legend, duly christened the Age of Monsters in reference to the colossal power of the cars they drove at record-breaking speeds for over a decade.

*Risking life and limb for a brief moment in time – the difference across a mile run between 150 mph (24 seconds per mile) and 180 mph (20 seconds per mile) is just 4 seconds.*

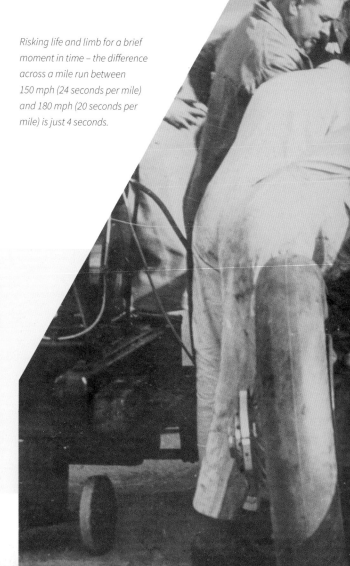

These two infamous British speed kings repeatedly vied with each other to secure the prestige of being the fastest man on earth – not only an accolade for themselves, but also an aspiration on behalf of their country. To boast the land speed record showered a country with global acclaim, celebrity glamour and an underlying reputation for engineering prowess; at a time of rising European tensions, that was a national boost not to be underestimated. Everyone involved proudly extolled the virtues of these land speed records for evolving engineering, discovering the best way forward for the sciences of aerodynamics, wind resistance, handling, tyres etc, and also any potential trickle-down effect for road-going cars and everyday engineering. This period is considered by many to be the glory days of land speed records.

Malcolm Campbell was born during the infancy of the motor car and as he grew up he became fascinated with engineering, as well as speed. Like the Red Devil, Camille Jenatzy, before him, as a young boy Campbell got his speed kicks on a bicycle, so much so that on one occasion he was fined 30 shillings for racing downhill with his hands off the handlebars!

This son of a Hatton Garden diamond seller developed an early passion for motorbikes and racing, including winning all three London to Land's End Trials motorbike races. Simultaneously he worked for Lloyds of London, initially for free, then for three years for as little as £1 a week. These early motorbike race wins were followed by success in cars at Brooklands.

Like many fellow racers, both Campbell and Segrave initially tested their mettle at that newly formed Surrey race circuit - indeed, at one point, the lap record there was also the world land speed record. However, when that ground-breaking track proved incapable of accommodating the ever-quickening speed machines, the circus moved on to narrow beaches and, later, the vast salt lakes that were to become the backdrop to some of the most remarkable and courageous of modern human endeavours.

After his early racing adventures, Campbell served in the First World War as a motorbike despatch rider, spending much of his time in the war serving in the Royal Flying Corps and later fighting at the Battle of Mons. Post-war, Captain Campbell dabbled in aviation challenges then began to carve out his place in land speed history. After racing a series of Darracq cars, including one that he found in a junk yard, he persuaded Wolverhampton's Sunbeam motor company to sell him a vehicle and renamed it Bluebird. The name was inspired by Maurice Maeterlinck's play, *The Blue Bird*, based on the story of a blue bird of happiness, which was said to be 'tantalizingly close, yet forever beyond reach'. The very same evening that Campbell read the play, he woke a paint shop owner up in the middle of the night to get the required colour ready in time to paint his vehicle for a race the following day at Brooklands. Legend has it that some parts of the bodywork's new paint job were still wet when Campbell began his first race the next morning.

*Admiring fans surround Sir Malcolm Campbell in his world famous Sunbeam land speed car.*

*Malcolm Campbell hitting 130 mph in June 1922.*

Campbell won two Grand Prix in a Bugatti T37A, but it was in the world of land speed that he would secure his legend. He had an inauspicious start with four failed attempts, including one where a tyre flew off his car and killed a spectator in the crowd (despite Campbell having allegedly asked organizers to move the spectators back to a safer distance). Then, in 1924, he finally broke the record for the first time, reaching 146.16 mph at Pendine Sands near Carmarthen Bay in south Wales, also in a Sunbeam. The 7-mile compacted stretch of sands at Carmarthenshire was so far under the motorsport radar that it didn't even feature in any guide books, but it turned out to be ideally suited to these speeding bullets. Campbell returned in 1925 and became the first person to achieve more than 150 mph – 150.87 mph, actually – in an even more powerful 350 hp V12 Sunbeam.

Campbell's great rival, Henry Segrave, born two years after the first ever race from Paris to Rouen, was the son of an Irish father and American mother. He became a First World War fighter pilot, was shot down twice in combat and would eventually be retired due to his wounds, with the parting words 'I always seem to make a mess of the landings!'

On leaving the RAF he had told his fellow servicemen he would soon travel faster than 200 mph - at a time when the world record was a measly 124 mph. After a successful career in motor racing, including becoming the first Briton to win a Grand Prix in a British car (the 1923 French GP, in a Sunbeam), Segrave retired from competitive racing to concentrate on land speed records.

*Campbell in his 450 bhp car ahead of a record attempt at Pendine Sands, alongside son Donald in his own toy racer.*

*Segrave's astonishing 1000 hp 'Mystery Racer' at Daytona.*

Above: The engineers and workers proudly unveil a land speed record monster.

Within two years, he had set his first record, 152.33 mph, on Southport Sands in a Sunbeam Tiger Ladybird. By this point, it was becoming apparent that road car engines were simply not going to suffice to keep moving the land speed record higher; physics tells us that power requirements increase as a cube of the speed, which means that, in real terms, if you are travelling at 100 mph but want to go 200 mph, you will need eight times the power, rather than just double. Where could they find such brute force? Simple - aeroplane engines! Segrave's Sunbeams were the first of a new era of aero-engined land speed cars, quite literally pulling engines out of aircraft, of which there was a convenient surplus following the end of hostilities.

In 1927, he went back to Sunbeam and developed with them what became known as the Mystery Racer, a giant but beautiful 1000 hp car, weighing four tonnes and complete with two aero engines, with Segrave sitting in between! The aluminium-bodied Sunbeam (designed by Captain Jack Irving) then went to the USA and became the first car to breach the 200 mph barrier, at 203.79 mph, thus proving his previous RAF speed prediction. This remarkable achievement was watched by over 30,000 people, and represented a huge jump in speed from his rival Campbell's previous benchmark of 174.88 mph. It would take road-going supercars six decades before they could match the same speed, and eighty years before that much power was embedded under a road car's bonnet. For one of the later runs, Segrave had to drive his car into the edge of the sea to cool the overheating brakes.

*Enthusiasts follow the Golden Arrow on Daytona Beach in 1929 as it prepares for a land speed record attempt.*

Perhaps Segrave's most famous record would be the 1929 land speed mark set in the stunningly beautiful, 925 hp, 27-litre Golden Arrow, championed by the founder of Castrol Oil and designed by J. S. Irving at a cost of around £10,000 (around £750,000 at the time of writing). The 3.5-tonne car even had a gunsight on the bonnet so that Segrave could accurately line up the track ahead. Remarkably, the golden car only had 18.74 miles on the clock when it achieved a record-breaking speed of 231.44 mph, watched by 12,000 spectators; the car took 6 minutes to turn around for the second run, and in this time Segrave's team had to repair a cooling system air cock that had been leaking and spraying his windscreen with steam and hot water. They also changed all four wheels,

because it was calculated that the Dunlop tyres could only last around 25 seconds at this top speed. Segrave announced his achievement by phoning his sponsors back in Britain over a newly established transatlantic telephone line, simply saying, in his magnificent English accent, 'Daytona calling, this is Segrave, she's done it!' Segrave returned to Britain a conquering hero and was promptly invited to Buckingham Palace and knighted, the first person to receive such an honour for his land speed exploits.

The Golden Arrow was never used again, leaving it with approximately just 36 miles on the clock, making it a car that was only used once, during which time it became the fastest vehicle to ever grace the Earth.

# Chapter 7

# Tempting Fate

*Our ambition at last achieved.*

Malcolm Campbell writing about becoming
the first person to surpass 300 mph

Segrave and Campbell needed to keep pushing, as they were not alone - their records were constantly under threat from each other, but also rivals such as Irishman Kenelm Lee Guinness (a former Isle of Man road racer who also invented the KLG spark plug); brilliant Welsh engineer J. G. Parry-Thomas, known as the Flying Celt (driving Babs, a second-hand, 27-litre V12 car based around an old lorry chassis and named after his mother); American Ray Keech, driving an 81-litre triple-engined monster called the White Triplex; Frank Lockhart in his Stutz Black Hawk, a very striking, low-profile bullet of a car that used two straight-eight racing engines twinned with a supercharged V16; and Lee Bible, one of Ray Keech's mechanics, who jumped into the hot seat when the latter refused to drive that particular car any more due to safety worries.

Several of these men - Bible, Lockhart and Parry-Thomas, for example - were killed in the process. Parry-Thomas' remarkable life is perhaps the most poignant of all these tragedies. This was actually the very first death in land speed circles: motor racing

had suffered fatalities before, but not land speed. Parry-Thomas had perennially battled against low budgets and an underdog status, but stunned the land speed elite with a number of astonishing records during this golden period, including raising the record from 152 mph to 170 mph, a massive leap forward against all the odds in his relatively crude but brutally swift car. However, events during one run in 1927 conspired against him before he even arrived at Pendine Sands. He had severe flu (possibly pneumonia) and had almost retired to his sick bed on the journey to south Wales, but was determined not to let his team down, so he carried on against doctor's advice and completed the trip to the venue in his open-top car. Contemporary photos show Parry-Thomas climbing into the cockpit wearing only a smart collared shirt, a diamond-patterned cardigan, goggles and a leather skullcap.

Feeling extremely unwell, Parry-Thomas began his record runs in his huge car, Red Slug, but struggled with his health and the difficult conditions. During a very quick run, one of the drive chains that powered

*Parry-Thomas refuelling for a record attempt in his car, Babs.*

*Parry-Thomas at Brooklands, 1925.*

his twin-aero engine snapped. The chain was situated outside the bodywork's metal cowling. Unfortunately, having raced many times on oval circuits, Parry-Thomas was in the habit of leaning out of the side of the cockpit and, according to some reports, he was in this exact position when the chain snapped, decapitating him instantly.

During a record attempt in the spring of 1928 at Daytona, Frank Lockhart's tyre is believed to have been slashed by a protruding seashell, leading to a fatal crash, with his body landing 50 feet from the wreckage, not far from his horrified wife. A year later at Ormond Beach in Florida, Lee Bible's car swerved and crashed, throwing him out and killing him

Parry-Thomas' tragic death in 1927 was the very first in the world of land speed records. His car, Babs, was buried under the sands of Daytona Beach. In the late 1960s, it was exhumed by a Wyn Owen who lovingly restored it, since when it has appeared at many classic race meetings. Subsequent investigations suggested that Parry-Thomas may have died from the rolling of the vehicle, rather than the catastrophic head injury reportedly sustained from the snapped drive chain.)

*Perhaps the most beautiful of all the land speed cars – Sir Henry Segrave's Golden Arrow. Note the huge crowds – in an era when only a handful of people could claim to be genuinely world famous, the land speed record was a surefire ticket to instant global celebrity and acclaim.*

*Benjamin '90*

as well as a Pathé News photographer that the vehicle hit. The USA would not capture the land speed record for another 34 years. One of the first men on the scene was Bible's good friend, Henry Segrave, who was so traumatized and saddened by the incident that he retired from land speed forever.

Although it was not in a land speed incident specifically, Kenelm Lee Guinness suffered severe head injuries in the 1924 San Sebastian Grand Prix, ending his racing career. In 1937, he was found dead aged just 49, an event the coroner reported as a suicide.

# WHEN A WOMAN MAKES HER WILL: Page 7

WIRELESS on PAGE 20

# DAILY SKETCH

*Modestina's Millinery* **BARGAINS**

No. 7,445. [Registered as a newspaper.]     THURSDAY, MARCH 2, 1933.     ONE PENNY.

## CAMPBELL PASSES THE POST
### *Bluebird's Record Dash*
### *That Thrilled the World*

The gamble with death won—that glorious first cigarette.

**THE SWELLING ROAR OF BLUE BIRD** drowning the noise of the waves as Sir Malcolm Campbell hurtled across Daytona Beach, past the timing stand.

These photographs are the first to reach England of Sir Malcolm Campbell when he broke his own world land speed record by 18.14 m.p.h. with an average speed of 272.108 m.p.h. Sir Malcolm, who is on his way home, speaking to members of the Empire Club, Toronto, predicted that at least 330 m.p.h. will be attained.

Malcolm Campbell's series of record-breaking
Bluebird machines are some of the most iconic
land speed vehicles of all time.

Despite these horrific accidents, the drivers chasing land speed records were almost universally undeterred. The speed breed enjoys going fast - and always faster - sometimes for the sake of it. This is one of the great tragedies in the history of speed, whereby many land speed racers have lost their lives trying to beat their own record. They are already the fastest ever, but that isn't enough. They have to keep pushing; it's a compulsion.

Across eleven years, Malcolm Campbell broke nine land speed records and, in 1932 and 1935 respectively, became the first person to surpass 250 mph and then 300 mph, latterly on the famous Bonneville Salt Flats in Utah, USA. By this point, the previously used locations such as Daytona were no longer big enough to accommodate the rapidly increasing top speeds and concurrent lengthy braking distances. For the magical 300 mph attempts, the by now 49-year-old Campbell used a new 36-litre, 2300 hp Bluebird. Even so, the odds were stacked against him - he suffered burst tyres, one of which caught fire; his windscreen was repeatedly soaked in oil, while his cockpit filled with toxic, acrid fumes. Yet he still managed to somehow record an average of 301.129 mph. Notably, for all of these record runs, Campbell - a very superstitious man - only ever got into the car on the same side and always carried with him a toy black cat that a lady had given him for good luck many years ago before a run at Brooklands.

Perhaps as much as any other early speed record, Campbell's final 301 mph achievement represents just how remarkable the progress of speed had been by the 1930s. For almost the first four decades of land speed record attempts, drivers had battled to reach the illustrious figures of 100 mph, then 150, then 200 and so on. Many felt that 300 mph was impossible, not just in terms of engineering but also regarding what the human body could cope with physically, and taking into account the number of factors that could go catastrophically wrong. When

# MASTER OF SPEED: SPECIAL MEMORIAL NUMBER

WIRELESS
PROGRAMMES
ON PAGE 20

# Daily Mirror
### THE DAILY PICTURE PAPER WITH THE LARGEST NET SALE

No. 8,290 | Registered at the G.P.O. as a Newspaper. | SATURDAY, JUNE 14, 1930 | One Penny

£750
BALLOT
FINAL
COUPON

# SEGRAVE KILLED IN BREAKING RECORD

Miss England II upside down after the crash. A rent can be seen in her hull.

Mr. C. Segrave (X), Sir Henry's father, arriving by air to go to his son's bedside yesterday.—(Pictures by "Daily Mirror" photo-telephony).

The three occupants of Miss England II at the time of the tragedy. (A to B), Mr. E. Halliwell, who was drowned, Sir Henry Segrave, and Mr. M. J. Willcocks, who was badly hurt.

Sir Henry Segrave, the holder of the world's land speed record, was killed on Lake Windermere yesterday during a successful attempt to wrest the world's water speed record from America. He set up new figures of 98.76 m.p.h. His 4,000-h.p. speedboat Miss England II turned turtle when travelling at terrific speed, and an explosion followed. She sank some time later. Sir Henry and a mechanic were pulled out of the water by people who rushed to the scene, and Sir Henry was taken to a house on the shore. Three doctors were summoned, but his multiple injuries proved fatal. He was thirty-four and received his knighthood last year. See also page 24.

Malcolm Campbell stunned the world in his glorious 301 mph Bluebird, it was a speed considered so high that a number of his land speed rivals simply gave up. The financial, emotional and personal cost of this record was so gargantuan an effort that to beat it was considered by some observers as being akin to climbing Everest.

This would be Campbell's last land speed record - he later switched disciplines and set several water speed records, such as the 141.74 mph in his Bluebird K4 on 19 August 1939, at Coniston Water. Unusually for speed demons from this era, Campbell died of a stroke and natural causes. By that time, 1948, he was aged 63. *Land Speed Records* author Liam McCann opines that 'Campbell's standing in the pantheon of speed kings is without equal'.

Segrave and Campbell were speed polymaths, breaking records on both land and water, a trait which would fade among speed merchants over the coming decades.

Henry Segrave, meanwhile, was prompted to retire from land speed after having seen his friend Lee Bible killed. However, Segrave could not quench his thirst for speed and so took to the water, initially inflicting a first defeat for nine years on the previously seemingly unbeatable motorboat racer, Garfield Wood (the first man to break 100 mph on water). Proving as capable on water as land, Segrave promptly captured the water speed record in Miss England II on the serene but often dangerous waters of Lake Windermere. However, on the following run, the boat is thought to have hit a log, capsizing and killing its mechanic. Segrave was pulled unconscious from the wreckage and rushed to hospital. Once there, he momentarily regained consciousness, immediately asked after the welfare of his men, was told that he had broken the water speed record, then passed away. His death was officially recorded as being caused by lung haemorrhages. In breaking the record, he also became the first man to hold both the land and water speed records simultaneously. When previously asked about why he had retired from his land speed record attempts, Segrave had prophetically said: 'I shall tempt fate no longer.'

# Chapter 8

# Bonneville

*Truly a place like no other. Pure white salt stretches out as far as the eye can see. It's so flat, and so smooth, it's almost as if you can see the curvature of the earth where the salt meets the horizon. This stunning piece of earth is fascinating to most people, but to speed freaks, including me, it's heaven on earth.*

Professional motorbike racer Elena Myers

As mentioned earlier, during the Age of Monsters the speeds were becoming so high that conventional race circuits simply could not accommodate these land bullets. A number of alternative venues were sourced, such as Pendine Sands, Daytona in Florida and, perhaps most famously of all, the Bonneville Salt Flats.

If any single location can claim to be inextricably linked to the history of land speed, it might just be Bonneville. It is a remote and peculiar location for any pursuit - west of the Great Salt Lake in western Utah, 80 miles from the nearest town of Wendover, the lake bed is boiling hot in summer and ultra-cold in winter, and is considered too barren for even the most simple of life forms to exist. Back in the early 1820s, explorer and trails man Joe Walker ominously warned visitors to these parts not to try to cross the salt beds because the journey was untried.

The salt lake's surface contains potassium, magnesium lithium and sodium chloride (common table salt) and can prove to be so salty that no vegetation will grow. Elsewhere, hardy plants and animals somehow survive near small ponds and marshy areas. Yet this dried-up prehistoric lake bed became a Holy Grail for the land speed record, that most demanding and complex of speed pursuits. The thick crust of salt that makes up its surface is baked solid by the searing sun and is said to help cool the wheels and tyres of these thundering speed machines. There is a tight window when the weather and geological gods are in a racer's favour, namely from the end of July until just before

*Sir Malcom Campbell's Bluebird car being towed onto the salt beds for a test run at Bonneville, September 1935.*

John Cobb with his serenely powerful Railton Special, clearly in his element in this special location, as F1 Operations manager Neil Waterman explains: 'Bonneville is all about romance! To any motorbike or car fan, it is all about romance. Speed week is a beautiful experience; with the right team it is phenomenal.'

the November snow (the world-famous Bonneville Speed Week takes place in August each year). The ethereal geology adds to the peculiar atmosphere, with mirages and the serene silence broken by these most extreme and ballistic of machines. How ironic that an area of 30,000 acres which has evolved so very little in millions of years has been home to some of the fastest vehicles on the planet. Peter Holthusen, writing in *Motorsport* magazine in April 2002, neatly summed up this location's unique strangeness, which is surely a metaphor for the extreme feats of the land speed crews: 'Bonneville Salt Flats is a door to the outer limits. A place of strangeness where almost anything can be imagined, almost anything can be achieved.'

Drag racer and women's motorbike land speed record holder Valerie Thompson finds Bonneville Speed Week an absolutely fascinating and life-affirming experience:

*It is just the most amazing place you can be on the planet. You see vehicles that have been crafted from people's garages, all these mavericks, these diamonds in the rough that are out there doing these crazy speeds. People have been going to Bonneville for decades, 10, 20, 30 years, going at it, just trying to go 150, 200, you know, there are people in their seventies going for senior world records who come back every year. We all share the same passion, the same enthusiasm, the same obsession with speed.*

Back in September 1938, it was on the Bonneville Salt Flats that another legend of the speed world would make a mark. The enigmatic John Cobb was born in 1899, the year after the first land speed record. He made his money as a director of a fur brokerage, which allowed him the funds to engage in large-capacity motor racing. He quickly showed a natural talent for speed by capturing the track record at Brooklands, reaching 143.44 mph in 1935, having snatched the mark from his friend Oliver Bertram. In mid-September 1938, John Cobb set the land speed record for the first time, driving the futuristic teardrop-shaped Railton Mobil Special to a speed of 350.2 mph.

Possibly one of the most striking and
unique of all the land speed monsters,
John Cobb's stunning Railton Special.

*Eyston's twin-engined Thunderbolt under
construction in the West Midlands, summer 1937.*

As seems to be the modus operandi for land speed, Cobb was relentlessly pushed by his rival and friend, Captain George Eyston. Inventor, engineer and racer, Eyston initially raced using a pseudonym when he was just a schoolboy. At Cambridge University he started boating, beginning his speed career in the water, racing motor boats. He served in the First World War and was awarded the Military Cross for his bravery, with the army noting he had exhibited 'conspicuous gallantry and devotion to duty, when carrying out reconnaissance ... under heavy shell and machine-gun fire'. He set a number of long-distance records, then jumped into Bugattis, winning races such as the 1926 French Grand Prix; later in his motorsport career he would become associated with racing MGs, such as the Magic Midget. The first signs of his land speed prowess arrived when he became one of the first Britons to run at Bonneville, setting new endurance records in his car, the Speed of the Wind. The peak came with his car Thunderbolt's trio of land speed records set between 1937 and 1939, the highest mark being his 357.5 mph in September 1938, a figure that lasted almost a year before John Cobb took it back in the Railton Special.

The cars at this stage were a mixture of supreme technology and the occasional old school oddity – for example, Eyston's 3200 hp Thunderbolt was push-started on its runs by a Ford Prefect saloon car, complete with reinforced front bumper, to avoid over-stressing the land speed car's transmission. By now, of course, these record speeds were far beyond anything that might be mirrored on the road. Specialist engines, vehicles and venues were a necessity, accompanied by potentially catastrophic risks. The escalating costs were now being met by sponsors, which also typified an era of commercialized land speed record attempts. Cobb's car was designed by Reid A. Railton, who had also designed Malcolm Campbell's Bluebird cars in the early 1930s. Like Campbell before him, Cobb was a staunch advocate of land speed engineering having a direct benefit for everyday engineering and motoring, and eagerly pushed for the improvement of road car oil and safer tyre technology, to name but two areas of interest.

George Eyston's beautiful Thunderbolt record car. Unusually for land speed racers of that era, Eyston lived into his eighties, passing away in 1979.

*Bonneville is sort of an eerie place. You feel all alone when you're on the salt. You look down that emptiness and it's just eerie as hell. It makes me uneasy.*

Art Arfons

Like Campbell and Segrave before them, the duo of Cobb and Eyston swapped the record several times in the mid-to-late 1930s, albeit not without incident. For example, when Eyston set the record at 311.42 mph in 1937, less than half an hour later rain started to fall, which instantly saw any further runs abandoned. On other runs, it transpired that it was impossible for the photo-electric timing equipment to distinguish his beautiful aluminium-bodied car from the bright sun-soaked salt surface of the dry lake, so the sides of the car were subsequently painted black.

George Eyston has a remarkable list of firsts to his name, including being the first person to complete 100 miles in one hour, to set the land speed record three times, and to break the world 1-hour record four times, the 12-hour record three times, the 24- and 48-hour record twice – and also the diesel record at 160 mph! As a director of Castrol Oil, Eyston was close to Cobb, and would later be part of the team working on the latter's ill-fated Crusader water speed attempt.

On 23 August 1939, Cobb pushed the mark up to 369.74 mph. Just nine days later, the Second World War was declared, and it would be a full eight years before Cobb's record was surpassed. During the war, Cobb himself served as a pilot in the RAF and later in the Air Transport Auxiliary, ultimately reaching the rank of Group Captain. With the onset of war, priorities shifted, and overnight speed for the sake of speed was deemed inappropriate. The stellar progress of the land speed demons and road-car pioneers immediately ground to a halt. For the moment, the irrepressible urge to go faster and faster appeared to have nowhere to go.

*Land speed has always captivated the general public and enjoyed a place in popular culture, such as here in this cigarette card illustration of George Eyston's Flying Spray, 1938.*

# Chapter 9

# Speed at War and in Recovery

*Dear killer, spare not thy sweet-cruel shot. A kind of grace it is to slay with speed.*

From *Astrophel and Stella* by Elizabethan poet and writer Sir Philip Sydney

When the world is at war, pouring money into a land speed record attempt or designing a high-end sports car is never going to be near the top of any nation's priorities. And so it was that between 1939 and 1945 the automobile and, by association, land speed barely progressed. In fact, during the Second World War, many parts of Western Europe observed much stricter speed regulations. For example, the British government ordered all car headlamps to be masked and streetlights turned off to avoid attracting enemy attacks from the skies, with the bizarre consequence that in the first six months of the war, fatalities on the roads (8272 in 1939) actually exceeded those caused by the actual fighting itself. Insurance companies were so concerned about the spike in accidents that a speed limit of just 20 mph was introduced for night-time driving (these deaths were not solely due to excessive speed, but generally poor driving conditions). Yet, by 1941, road deaths had risen by 38 per cent, even though there were half the number of cars on the road in that year than before the war started.

British Double Summer Time was then introduced, in part to help reduce the rising death toll.

There were other circumstances of war that diluted the chance for speed to evolve in everyday life. In many countries, driving tests were suspended so there was no new flush of drivers to buy any cars, let alone quicker ones; petrol was rationed (in Britain to around just 200 miles per car per month); road infrastructure projects were put on ice; and, more generally, raw materials and factories were commandeered to furnish the war effort. Car manufacture pretty much ceased as industrial resources were used to manufacture aircraft, tanks, war vehicles, bombs, torpedoes, steel helmets, ammunition and other military materials. It wasn't just car resources that were redirected - for example, lingerie companies made parachute netting and cash register companies manufactured rifles.

However, necessity being the mother of invention, speed *did* dramatically evolve during the war years - in engineering.

The need for rapid manufacture meant that factory processes were refined at lightning speed – for example, the Kaiser's shipyards were able to reduce the time for a ship to be built from one year to 62 days or less. Capacity in Western Europe's factories rocketed, unemployment was slashed and national productivity of the major economies blossomed. Though this did not directly influence society's relationship with speed at the time, the multiple and significant leaps forward in engineering would soon catapult the science behind speed into a new age.

Specific to the history of speed, the war years saw a number of innovations that would ultimately generate ever higher speeds once the conflict was over, both on the road and in speed-focused vehicles. Power steering meant that heavy military vehicles could be manoeuvred easily and quickly; fuel injection systems were massively refined for aircraft engines and would eventually find their way into road-going vehicles; the long-standing technology of superchargers was updated for a new use, in aeroplanes that were struggling to operate at top speeds in the thin air of high-altitude combat; the increased use of plastics made military vehicles lighter and more flexible; and manufacturing processes were refined so much that lighter, cheaper and – of more relevance here – *faster* machines were successfully being designed and manufactured.

The decade or so after the war was a pivotal period in the history of speed, for multiple reasons. It was in these post-war years that speed re-emerged as a major – and arguably quintessential – element of modern society. Initially, the sense of liberation and celebration at the end of hostilities was obviously immense, but the economic reality lurking behind the joyous street parties and smiling politicians was rather more savage. The Allies had won the war, but many of those countries were essentially bankrupted; British national debt peaked in the late 1940s at over 230 per cent of GDP. And, of course, Germany, formerly an industrial powerhouse and hub of

*Luigi Chinetti passes the pits in his Ferrari 166MM at Le Mans in 1949. Two years later, the all-women team of Betty Haig and Yvonne Simon came fifteenth overall at Le Mans in a Ferrari 166 MM Coupé – yet it would be another twenty years until another woman competed at that famous race.*

automotive ingenuity, was now derelict. Across Europe, obliterated factories had to be rebuilt and retooled, so it was some time before the automobile industry got back on its feet. Even then, the automotive culture was for frugal, economical cars, not speed machines. Any post-war rebirth of speed was further delayed by some European countries imposing taxes and petrol rationing for many years to come. This was a time when the public's perception of speed was most definitely not through

road cars - models such as the Renault 4CV, Citroën 2CV, Morris Minor, Fiat 500C and the Volkswagen Beetle were never going to get the adrenaline coursing. There were a few notable exceptions: the Corvette debuted in 1953, the Jaguar XK120 was the world's fastest road car for a time, and Aston Martin produced some delightful mechanical works of art; lightweight materials made cars such as the J1 Allard much faster and, of course, in 1949 Ferrari's 166 Inter heralded that famous marque's entrance into the world of road-going speed. There was also a vogue for turning race-winning cars into road-going versions, such as the Ferrari 375MM and 250S plus the Porsche 550 that James Dean crashed and died in.

In the USA, factories had been geographically cocooned from the air raids, and although the war effort had naturally still taken a toll, the USA bounced back stronger and more quickly than Europe. Even so, speed was often last on the list of American car makers' priorities when developing new vehicles. Delmar Roos, chief engineer of US car maker Willys-Overland had previously said: 'The object of the automobile is to transport a given number of people in reasonable comfort, with the least consumption of gasoline, oil and rubber, and for the slightest operating cost and prime price.'

However, there were certain features of post-war life that encouraged modern society's seemingly unquenchable need for speed. Although the commercial demand for fast cars would remain muted for some years to come, the technology to produce such machines had enjoyed the wartime turbo-boost in machining, engine technology, tyre manufacture, factory systems and so on, which over the coming years would become increasingly available for commercial exploitation. Further, with the military's brilliant engineering minds no longer needed for the war effort, many of them were snapped up by industries such as shipbuilding and car manufacture. And there were plenty of opportunities to test their new, faster ideas - for example, across Britain the majority of wartime airfields were now redundant, and these flat, open spaces provided the basis for the birth of modern British motorsport in an explosion

of speed that is still resonating to this day and perhaps represents one of the greatest legacies of war for speed.

The decade after the war did see an enormous growth of sports car sales. Advancing manufacturing technology was bringing costs down each year and, in so doing, increasing the possibility of owning a nimble car that wasn't just a daily drive. That said, these cars were still beyond the financial reach of many, not least because their small size and relative lack of practical features meant that sports cars were often the owner's second car - in the post-war years, a significant luxury - rather than the sole family vehicle.

However, perhaps more than for any other reason, the ten years or so after the war was crucial to this story not because of developments on the race track or in the factories of motor manufacturers around the world, but instead on public roads and in the youth subcultures of both Britain and the USA. Firstly, although this book does not extend to a comprehensive history of speed on motorbikes, there is an absolutely imperative diversion into a British two-wheeled world to explain this pivotal phase of society's wider experience - and perception - of speed: the Ton Up Boys of the 1950s.

A quick rewind into history tells us that the motorbike boasts a long and hugely colourful history. As far back as the mid-Victorian era, steam power had been toyed with for two-wheeled machines, essentially by strapping a steam engine

*The coolest outsiders – the so-called 'Ton Up Boys' of the 1950s were one of the earliest subcultures who took the pursuit of speed underground.*

onto a primitive bicycle, the velocipede! The first petrol-fuelled, internally combusted motorbike came in 1885, the same year as Benz's famous Motorwagen. That bike, the Daimler Reitwagen, was designed by Benz's contemporaries, Gottlieb Daimler and Wilhelm Maybach, in Germany. A rival machine made by Hildebrand and Wolfmuller was produced in 1894, which marked the start of series-produced motorbikes. The First World War proved the motorbike to be an invaluable tool for modern mobility, and since then the two-wheeler has been a literal and symbolic bastion of individual freedom, being cheaper than the equivalent car, and easier to use and store. The history of two-wheeled speed is fascinating, but obviously deserves a lengthy study in its own right.

However, hugely relevant to this history of speed is the role of the motorbike in the society of the 1950s, specifically here the Ton Up Boys. Also known as Cafe Racers, this very early modern youth subculture

*Opposite: Ton Up Boys, or Cafe Racers as they were also known, prided themselves on being able to modify their motorbikes themselves, without the need for professional help.*

is crucial to the history of speed for four reasons: their sheer, unadulterated passion for going fast; the aesthetic they created; the social reaction – and in many cases revulsion – that their very existence generated; and the consequence of wrenching speed away from the privileged few, creating a democratization of speed.

By the 1950s, post-war Britain began to enjoy a renewed prosperity, and with this growing economic stability came a new availability of credit and finance for young people. Do youngsters on the fringes of society use credit to buy sensible housing or make solid investments in the financial markets?

Of course not! They go and buy the coolest, fastest motorbike or car they can afford. And in the world of two wheels there were plenty of options, as British bike companies were certainly enjoying race success all over the world. Triumph in particular enjoyed glory days during this period, but marques such as Norton, BSA, AJS, Matchless et al were also hugely popular. Latter-day race replicas were not available at this point, so admiring youngsters started to modify their own machines themselves. Their bikes were not redesigned for superficial looks but just for sheer speed. Parts such as mirrors and fairings were stripped off, handlebars dipped down and engines highly tuned.

# Daily Mirror

2½d. Thursday, February 9, 1961 • • • No. 17,775

**SHOCK ISSUE** **SHOCK ISSUE..**

# SUICIDE CLUB!

- It devours 130,000 members EVERY YEAR ! !
- See Pages 3, 13, 14, 15 and 28 today ! ! !

This group of young motorbike fanatics began to congregate at many of the cafes that were appearing on the newly arterial roads around much of Britain. Most famous of these was the Ace Cafe situated on London's North Circular Road, a new road loop around the capital that offered many long, smooth stretches ideal for fast riding. Often these young men would race between the cafes, with the optimum aim of hitting the magical 100 mph mark - the ton - hence the name Ton Up Boys. The Ace was being replicated around Britain by hundreds of cafes where the Ton Up Boys would socialize, chat, listen to rock 'n' roll on the jukebox (it was not yet widely on the radio) and tinker with their bikes. A modern-day motorbike would, of course, obliterate the Cafe Racer's speed capabilities, but in the 1950s these rapid modified bikes were a revelation. They were (relatively) affordable, too – a crucial separation for the lower classes from the eye-watering costs of production performance cars.

At this time, society was undertaking one of its most significant cultural transformations – the arrival of the teenager. The newborn teen no longer existed by the edict that young people were just copycat versions of their parents - quite the opposite. Clothes, music, transport, language and lifestyle now all became fiercely independent of parental influence, deliberately so. Most obviously, teenagers looked to the new religion of rock 'n' roll for their kicks, which in those very early years came with a large dose of Americana.

The cultural impact of American music and movies on British teenagers was massive, as stars such as Buddy Holly, Elvis Presley and Chuck Berry dominated jukeboxes, while youths crammed into cinemas (and sometimes rioted outside them) to watch films such as *Rock Around The Clock*. Along with the greater availability of credit, these factors all created a perfect storm for a new generation of speed freaks. Most relevant to the Ton Up Boys and the history of speed was 1953's *The Wild Ones* starring Marlon Brando as the leather-clad Johnny Strabler. This seminal subculture classic about a band of outlaw bikers rampaging across US towns horrified mainstream USA; in Britain, the film wasn't even shown until fifteen years later, surfacing in around 1968 when photographs from the American release of the film were circulated in newspaper reports. This influence was reflected in the standard Ton Up Boy appearance, which was a striking aesthetic. The look was initially one borne out of practicality, but has since become a hugely revered and popular sartorial style: leather-clad and monochrome, with slicked back hair often shaped into a so-called D.A., or duck's arse, sweep at the rear, tall and hefty biker boots, the staple leather jacket, open-faced helmet and goggles (often no helmet at all), white silk scarf and T-shirt. However, first and foremost this potent youth subculture was about speed. This provocative subculture was matched by an equally establishment-baiting new tribe across the Atlantic.

# Chapter 10

# Speeding from the
# Underground

*A cult of backyard mechanics, utilising junkyard parts, create streamlined no-nonsense racing machines for competition over straight-line courses, laid out locally or on nearby desert flats.*

John Carroll and Garry Stuart in *The Ultimate Guide to Hot Rods*

*Hot Rod is the oldest magazine devoted to the genre, being first published in January 1948.*

The Ton Up Boys had spiritual cousins across the Atlantic, in a second striking example of how 1950s teenage rebellion sought out speed as the oxygen of its very existence: hot rods. Originating back in 1930s Prohibition-era USA, hot rods were heavily modified road cars capable of great speeds, initially to help bootleggers evade law enforcement. Early races were held on dry lake beds with increasing regularity such that, by the late 1940s, this scene was hugely popular among younger speed freaks. Analogous with the Cafe Racer bikes, hot rods were relatively affordable, given that the donor cars were most often older vehicles such as Ford Model Ts and Model As, which were plentiful and therefore reasonably cheap, as well as being easy to self-modify. Engine swaps were commonplace, such as mounting large V8s into these tiny shells, creating blistering speed potential. Again, like the Ton Up Boys, hot rod owners stripped their vehicles of all peripheral items to reduce weight, while bodywork was frequently channelled and sculpted to create unique and eye-catching cars.

*The first generation of teenagers found music, fashion and speed a compelling way to separate themselves from their elders.*

Again, as in Britain, disused airfields provided early hot rod fanatics with the space to hit top speeds away from the public roads. This would eventually lead to the creation of the National Hot Rod Association (the world of drag racing will be examined later in this book). Public interest was sufficiently rabid that the magazine *Hot Rod* was founded as far back as 1948. The place of hot rods in American popular culture was later assured, with revered writers such as Tom Wolfe covering the scene in his collection of essays, *The Kandy-Kolored Tangerine-Flake Streamline Baby*.

The British and American speed teens were not alone – the international reach of speed's appeal to the teenager during the 1950s was massive. At the tail-end of the 50s, a teenager called Gordon Murray was growing up in Durban, South Africa, and just starting to become obsessed with going fast. Gordon's dad had been a chauffeur, then a motor mechanic who would eventually work for the South African Air Force during the war, so oily fingernails were in the family blood.

*For many Americans, hot rods were an essential part of 1950s teenage life.*

Gordon was a surfer with a twin passion for rock 'n' roll and speed, an obsession that, a generation later and in a world of multi-million-dollar precision engineering, would eventually see him design the iconic McLaren F1, now considered by many as the greatest supercar of all time.

Back in the simpler times of 1950s Durban, the teenage Murray was completely fascinated by motor cars, the faster the better:

*The view from behind the starting line at a National Hot Rod Association (NHRA)-sponsored drag race at the Orange County Airport runway, California, March 1957.*

People didn't really have much money after the war to buy or race cars, so they built what were known as 'specials'. In South Africa anyway, the only supercars were really handmade specials. If you've seen George Lucas's film, American Graffiti ... that's my upbringing, drive-in movies, milk shake bars, the music, the style, all that. There was one such milk shake bar called The Nest on North Beach and people that owned (and/or liked) hot cars used to gather there every Sunday night, all the bonnets would be up and there would be loads of people picking fights.

Like their Ton Up Boy cousins across the Atlantic, US hot rodders prided themselves on extensive, home-built modifcations.

*Seminal motorsport and supercar designer Gordon Murray working as a teenager on his first ever build.*

It was in this testosterone-fuelled atmosphere that Murray's genius began to germinate:

*I was into bikes and cars and I raced, of course. I had a '56 Hillman Minx because that was all my dad could afford. I didn't care, I immediately modified it by taking the hub caps off, I painted the wheels silver and added a noisy exhaust and I used to drive around with the choke pulled out so it sounded like it was tuned. That's all I could afford but in that mob there were some serious cars. They all used to tune Fords in those days, Anglias and Cortinas that people would put 1650 engines in, Weber carbs, and they would be pretty quick little cars. However, there were a couple of cars such as an AC Ace that I can remember seeing for the first time and thinking, Bloody hell! That's quick! There weren't a lot of Porsches or E-Types or Ferraris, nothing like that in South Africa, really, that I was aware of. Possibly in Johannesburg where the money was, but certainly not in Durban which was sort of a Blackpool, seaside, summer holiday place where I don't remember anything exotic until that particular AC Ace. The owner used to race it in the Tongar Burns races and it was properly quick. The whole environment was just so intoxicating and left an indelible mark on my mind.*

*Teenage drive-in movie and milkshake bar fanatic Gordon Murray's prodigious engineering and design brain would later create the McLaren F1, regarded by many as the greatest supercar of all-time.*

Clearly these clusters of Ton Up Boys, hot rod racers and international speed merchants scattered all around the world looked and sounded very different given their geographical distance and cultural differences, but they all had much in common. These scenes were widely reviled by the mainstream, crudely summarized as antisocial and violent, and tagged as unwelcome social pariahs. Of course, these outlaw crowds often did have elements that justified a degree of legal or cultural disapproval, but in general they were the subject of widespread prejudice. Reports of fighting, drinking and antisocial behaviour were frequently heavily exaggerated by the media and scowled upon by an unimpressed mainstream society. This conventional revulsion and even hysteria in response to such outlaw fringes would later be replicated with other subcultures such as mods, rockers and punks, and was chronicled perfectly in Stan Cohen's definitive 1973 study, *Folk Devils and Moral Panics:*

*The deviant or group of deviants is segregated or isolated and this operates to alienate them from conventional society. They perceive themselves as more deviant, group themselves and others in a similar position and this leads to more deviance. ...*

*More moral panics will be generated and other, as yet nameless folk devils will be created ... our society as present structured will continue to generate problems for some of its members - like working class adolescents - and then condemn whatever solution these groups find.*

Pivotally, Britain's Ton Up Boys and the hot rod kids in the USA changed forever the standard perception of speed. Previously, speed had been the domain of the wealthy, of glamour, of privilege. The land speed kings and motor-racing heroes were perceived as other-worldly, almost superhuman figures, while road-going speed was obtainable only to those with significant incomes and high-class backgrounds. The new existence of these visually distinctive teenagers tearing around public roads, causing neighbourhood curtains to twitch and police patrols to pounce, suddenly made speed a society-scaring alternative way of life. These were outlaws both on the road and in their lifestyle. These youngsters took speed out of the hands of the elite and thrust it into the world of the person in the street, democratizing the thrill of going

fast for *everyone*. Subsequently, speed was no longer the preserve of the wealthy, but an experiential commodity finally within the reach of the lower classes. On that basis, although the 1950s saw little absolute progress in the traditional world of speed, this societal sea-change in terms of a wider accessibility to going fast made the decade perhaps the single most important moment in the modern story of speed.

Over three decades later, Durban lad Gordon Murray would draw on his own formative teenage experiences in the 1950s when, having established himself as one of the most successful Formula 1 designers of all time, he set out to create the greatest driver's car the world had ever seen, commissioned by a racing team that had never previously manufactured a road car: a project that would come to be known as the McLaren F1. In 1995, this fabled supercar, a watershed pinnacle of pure speed, became the fastest production car ever, hitting 240 mph and later becoming the first road car to win at Le Mans since the 1940s, an achievement of engineering brilliance and pure speed that will most likely never be repeated. And Murray's only regret? That the McLaren F1 hadn't been driven to and from Le Mans for the race in the vivacious style of the glorious Gentlemen Racers of the 1920s.

See what happens when you let a bunch of teenagers tinker with fast cars?

# Chapter 11

# The
# Jet Age

*I want to break the record. This is my life; this is what I chose; it's the only thing I know. If I don't make the record, down deep I'm glad because I didn't have to push Arthur [Arfons]. I'm afraid for him. He'd throw all precautions to the wind. I wouldn't want nothing to happen to him.*

Walter Arfons, half of the famous land speed Arfons brothers

If performance automobile manufacture stalled during the war years and arguably for a decade afterwards, one area of engineering that certainly did not stagnate during this period was aeronautics. For obvious military reasons, the war had been a period of massive development across all types of aircraft, not just fighter planes. The First World War had seen a high-profile but relatively modest role for aircraft, but by the time of the 1939-1945 conflict, aeroplanes were considered by many to be the single most important weapons delivery system. Both Germany and Japan launched their campaigns with heavy airstrikes, so from the very opening of hostilities all the combatants knew their air tech had to be the best, meaning that the very finest engineering brains were immediately commandeered for the war effort. The Spitfire is a famous example of the engineering response to this greater airborne threat, the Battle of Britain its apex. These flying machines were almost unrecognizable from their First World War counterparts - gone were the wood-and-fabric biplanes, replaced by streamlined cantilevered monoplanes constructed from aluminium airframes with ferocious, frequently supercharged, piston engines. At the start of the war, the typical engine produced around 1000 hp; by the end of hostilities, that had doubled.

This rapid development would ultimately become crucial in the history of speed down on the ground. Although the majority of aerial battles were fought by propeller-driven, human-piloted fighters and bombers, one of the most radical new innovations during the war years was the jet-powered aircraft; towards the end of the war, rocket engines were also being trialled by various countries. Although the number of actual combat missions completed by these revolutionary aircraft was relatively modest, in terms of new methods of propulsion for speed freaks the game was about to change beyond all recognition. The secretive wartime engineers behind these new technologies had effectively provided the engineering to produce land speed record vehicles that were more akin to missiles than anything else.

In the world of post-war land speed, progress was initially muted. Record attempts were scarce and the key players relatively inactive, save for a blistering record of 394.196 mph by John Cobb in his Mobil-sponsored Railton Special in the autumn of 1947, including the world's first single pass in excess of 400 mph.

Between 1945 and 1963, this would remain the solitary new land speed record. Indeed, this speed lull is as notable for Cobb's tragic death as for the lack of new records. The famous record breaker died in 1952 on Loch Ness, attempting a new water speed record. Running at 30 mph above the existing record, his jet boat Crusader hit an unexpected wake, bounced, nosedived then broke into pieces, violently throwing Cobb from the cockpit. He survived but was badly injured and died of

*Despite the surface of Bonneville being in very poor condition, the famously courageous John Cobb hit a top speed of 415 mph during his 1947 record runs.*

heart failure shortly after. The Pathé News announcing his death said that he had died 'Fighting as always, to win new glories for Britain. The glories that he had won during his lifetime were not for himself, but for his country. He was above all, a great Englishman.' In recognition of his famous courage and efforts, Cobb was posthumously awarded the Queen's Commendation for Brave Conduct in March 1953, 'for services in attempting to break the world's water speed record, and in research into high speed on water'.

Cobb's final land speed record, meanwhile, just over 5 mph short of the 400 mph mark, remained untouched for nearly seventeen years; with his death, and amidst little enthusiasm for new record attempts, it felt like the era of land speed had also passed. However, the human instinct to be the very fastest on earth appears to be inextinguishable, such that, when land speed exploded back into life in the early 1960s, it did so at a hugely quicker rate, with the onset of an insanely fast new generation of jet cars.

The first jet-powered land speed car, Flying Caduceus, was driven by Dr Nathan Ostich at Bonneville in the summer of 1960. The car did not break any records, but it did signal a changing of the guard in the land speed world. Then American hot-rodder Craig Breedlove entered the land speed arena. He was the son of a special effects supervisor and a studio dancer, and he had started modifying cars aged just thirteen, drag-racing them as soon as he reached the

legal age of sixteen – not long after hitting 154 mph at Bonneville in a Ford hot rod he had built himself. At the age of just twenty, he registered 236 mph in a streamlined Oldsmobile. Breedlove was a natural, and few land speed competitors were surprised when he then appeared to beat John Cobb's existing record by 13 mph, moving the mark up to 407.477 mph in his jet-engined vehicle Spirit of America (even though it only used 90 per cent of available thrust!). However, Breedlove's speed was initially not ratified by the Fédération Internationale de l'Automobile (FIA) on two grounds: his vehicle had had only three wheels (not the required four) and the jet engine did not drive the axles as it should have, in another established criterion.

The beginning of the end for the wheel-driven, petrol-engined land speed car came in August 1960 when Donald Campbell, son of the land speed legend, launched a record bid in his expensive and much-heralded car, the massive 30-foot-long, near-9000 lb CN7 Bluebird. Campbell had worked as a travelling salesman in the City of London, as a maintenance engineer in Essex and then in a company manufacturing power tools, before developing a fascination with boats that would ultimately see him gain several water speed records. However, when he ran the CN7, he suffered a horrific high-speed crash that saw his skull fractured and his car severely damaged. But for the car's incredibly strong structure, Campbell would surely have perished. Undeterred by his own injuries and the recent death of another land speed competitor (Athol Graham), Donald announced from his hospital bed that he would soon make another attempt on the alluring 400 mph mark in Bluebird.

This record attempt was not without huge pressure on Donald - the car had cost £900,000, almost four times more than Breedlove's machine, so there was intense expectation, not least due to such an enormous investment. Campbell sensed the new generation of jet-powered cars were about to rewrite the speed record books, yet bad weather and engineering challenges all stifled his progress. However, despite fighting rising flood waters and a lake surface that was beginning to break up, Donald was not to be beaten. In the summer of 1964, he finally matched his father's achievement (having always lived in his shadow to some degree), by posting what would become the last wheel-driven land speed record, hitting 403.1 mph in Bluebird on Lake Eyre in Australia - in true land speed style, he was reportedly disappointed, as the car had been designed to hit 500 mph! Nonetheless, he became the first person to surpass the 400 mph mark across two runs, or 6.66 miles a minute. However, the jet-powered racers were now in town and Campbell's record would only stand for a few months. In December 1964, Donald Campbell did something that not even his famous father had achieved - he broke the water speed record, on Lake Dumbleyung, making him the only man to ever hold both land and water speed records in the same calendar year, a feat he achieved with just nine hours to spare!

Less than three years later, Donald Campbell made an attempt on the world water speed record, aiming for 300 mph, on Coniston Water. After a successful high-speed run, his Bluebird set out on a second pass, but left the water, completed a near-somersault and smashed into the surface of the lake, cartwheeling to a halt. Campbell was killed and although his helmet was recovered from the accident, his body was not located and removed from the lake until 2001.

*'Before long my husband may be the fastest man on earth, or I may be a widow.' Donald Campbell's third wife, Tonia Bern. Donald was killed on Coniston Water in January 1967. His radio transcript gave a horrifying insight into his demise: 'I can't see much and the water is very bad indeed … I'm galloping over the top … and she's giving a hell of a bloody row here … I can't see anything, I'm having to draw back … I've got the bows up … I'm going … oh!'*

*Campbell's daughter Gina was just seventeen years old when her father died. In 2001, her father's body was recovered from the lake, and found nearby was his mascot, a small brown teddy bear called Mr Whoppit; Gina still has this cherished heirloom.*

*One of the history of speed's most inspirational and exceptional personalities, American speed king Craig Breedlove – seen here celebrating becoming the first person to pass 600 mph, in November 1965.*

During this first age of jet-powered land speed, controversy grabbed as many headlines as the speeds themselves, because the debate raged about what did and did not constitute a land speed vehicle. Alongside Breedlove's, other cars such as part-time stock car racer and engineer Tom Green's Wingfoot Express and former naval mechanic Art Arfons' Green Monster also posted high numbers (the former taking Campbell's record just seventy-eight days later). However, there was a period of intense debate over who actually held the land speed record, with various categories vying for the crown. The FIA chose to simplify matters in December 1964 when they announced that the record would be held by whichever vehicle posted the absolute top speed, regardless of whether it was wheel-driven or not. Overnight, the potential for the record exploded ... what came over the next half-century of speed chasing would prove to be quite astonishing.

Similar to the Campbell family's Bluebird trait, all of speed king Craig Breedlove's machines are called Spirit of America. In the history books of land speed, Breedlove's name is an icon: he was the first man to pass both 500 mph and 600 mph. The former speed was surpassed when he hit 526.277 mph in a $250,000 car in October 1964, although the record attempt was not without incident. After completing one particular run, Breedlove released the drogue parachutes designed to slow his vehicle down, but one of the shroud lines snapped off, leaving him with just disc brakes that were only designed to stop the car once it was under 200 mph. The absence of sufficient stopping power sent his car careering off *for five miles,* before eventually smashing into a row of telephone poles, snapping one off, then bouncing across a small road, eventually coming to rest nose first in a salt pond with the vehicle's tail sticking in the air. Incredibly, Breedlove was unharmed, and as marshals raced over to check he was okay, he quipped: 'And for my next trick, I'm going to set myself on fire!' Initially, the FIA refused to ratify it because it was a three-wheeler, so instead the Fédération Internationale de Motorcyclisme (FIM) acknowledged the record, despite Breedlove never intending the machine to be regarded as a motorbike.

*Craig Breedlove is a fascinating character – reportedly he worried about his beloved wife driving on public roads above 75 mph then encouraged her to try the Spirit of America Sonic 1, in which she set a women's record of 308.56 mph. The Breedloves remain the fastest couple ever!*

In true land speed style, Breedlove was pushed constantly by rival record racers. Just twelve days after Breedlove's 500 mph+ mark had been set, Art Arfons broke the record by 10 mph in his Green Monster. The son of a chickenfeed farmer from Akron, Ohio, Art had movie-star good looks and bravery to match, yet the superstitious hero insisted that all his crew members should kiss the car every day. So inventive was he with low budgets and high-speed engineering that some peers called him 'the junkyard genius of the jet set'. The Green Monster had parts from a 1937 Lincoln, pre-war Packard steering and a Ford truck axle. He even rigged a shotgun up to fire off the parachutes, and hand-built the original body for just $1000. The engine was picked up in Miami, having been listed as suffering from 'foreign object damage' and bought for just $625. The car cost $10,000 in total, compared to the $250,000 spent on Breedlove's Spirit of America.

Like many land speed competitors, Art was not without his own near-misses. On the record run he suffered a tyre blow out at around 575 mph and his cockpit filled with acrid, blinding smoke – but Art simply smashed the cabin window so he could see well enough to steer his charging ride back on course, then pulled the manual lever to open his chutes and decelerate to safety. A representative from his sponsor Firestone explained how unbelievably calm and collected their driver was at that life-threatening moment of disaster:

*Blowouts don't bother Art ... he didn't panic. He hit the kill button on his steering wheel; this shut down the engine and he coasted to about 500 miles an hour. Then he popped his first chute and it went all to pieces and jerked the car real bad. He just held onto the steering till the car straightened out, and then he popped the other chute at about 400 and it tore in two, but it slowed him down and at 350 he hit the brakes and burned them out, and he just rode it down on three wheels.*

Art Arfons would need all his famous powers of calm and courage when he returned to Bonneville another time with a modified Green Monster – while the car was travelling at around 610 mph, a wheel bearing seized, sending the car into a barrel roll then a cartwheel, coming to rest after 4.5 miles. Art emerged with only cuts to his face.

The race was relentless between these fierce speed rivals. Breedlove's next car, the Spirit of America Sonic 1, was a four-wheeler, powered by a 15,000 lbs thrust afterburning J79 turbojet, and first averaged 555.485 mph; yet Arfons and the Green Monster hit back even more rapidly just five days later, adding over 20 mph. During this one remarkable period alone, the land speed record had been broken five times in 25 days, and increased by an astonishing 123.51 mph. The intense rivalry was heightened because tyre manufacturers Goodyear and Firestone were backing competing cars, further commercializing and ramping up the race to be the fastest – which also displays how the world of business believed that the land speed record still had a commercial value in the eyes of the public.

Land speed legend Richard Noble has very fond memories of both these famous racers:

*Art was brilliant, just a really nice guy. [Years later] he came over to the UK with his family to see ThrustSSC in build and spent some time with us. On the first day we went and found John Cobb's widow at her flat in London. Art was heavily influenced by Cobb and so when he met his wife, Art just went kind of soggy at the knees, he was thrilled to meet her and he was a real gentleman. Then we went down to Sussex to see ThrustSSC being built and Art was absolutely amazed. He pored over it, looking at every single weld, every nut and every bolt on the structure and got very, very excited.*

*Breedlove is very different to Arfons. Art was a very quiet, deep thinker and very clever.*

*Breedlove is an incredibly brave guy and an amazing engineer. Over the years he had all sorts of really appalling accidents yet was quite happy travelling at 600 mph with the front of the car in the air! He is also an exceptional communicator, with a great sense of humour and always a genuine challenger. Both these men were the greatest competitors of that age.*

In November 1965, Breedlove became the first person to break the 600 mph barrier, but his first run only managed to hit around 595 mph, meaning his second run would have to average a much higher speed to set the aggregate record. This is exactly what he did, hitting a remarkable 608.201 mph on the final run, thus setting a new record of 601.601 mph. 'That 600 is about a thousand times better than 599,' he said afterward. 'Boy, it's a great feeling.' That astounding mark would remain unbeaten until 1970.

The first jet-engined era also marked a shift across the Atlantic in terms of the speed crown. Whereas between 1914 and 1964 nine different British drivers had held the land speed record, there was only the solitary American Ray Keech (along with one record by Frenchman René Thomas) breaking up that dominance. In that period, the record rocketed from 124.09 to 403.1 mph.

However, once the regulations were altered to allow non-wheel-driven cars, a new era of American dominance began. After Breedlove's battles with Arfons and Tom Green in search of 600 mph, fellow American Gary Gabelich entered the fray. Former delivery driver

Gary Gabelich's The Blue Flame was literally a rocket on wheels and scooped the land speed record in the autumn of 1970, hitting 622.407 mph.

Gabelich had raced his father's Pontiac while still at school, then enrolled as a part-time test subject for the Apollo space programme, while also pursuing a successful amateur pastime of drag racing. As soon as he turned his attention to land speed, it became apparent that he was a very gifted competitor. His 1970 The Blue Flame was the first rocket dragster propelled by hydrogen peroxide and liquefied natural gas, pressurized with helium gas (its name was inspired by the use of natural gas fuel). This very slender 38-foot pencil-shaped car was reported to boast 35,000 hp, equivalent to 37 megawatts, but at full thrust that insane amount of power was accessible for just 20 seconds. The apocalyptic new propulsion system clearly worked – Gabelich set a new record of

622.407 mph across the measured mile; this made the car the first ever vehicle to surpass 1000km/h. Gabelich, now the fastest man on earth, was actually a replacement for the original driver, Chuck Suba, who had sadly been killed in a dragster accident.

As the jet era evolved, new innovations such as aluminium wheels removed the need for tyres; exploding or deteriorating rubber had been the cause of many failed attempts and fatalities over the years, so this was a significant moment in the sport.

There seemed no end to the sheer courage/madness of these amazing individuals. When the team behind the Budweiser Rocket realized that their car needed more thrust – despite already being powered by a Romance R4 rocket - they strapped the propulsion system from a Sidewinder missile onto the vehicle to add another 600 lbs of thrust! Although not qualifying fully with the regulations, this car was then claimed to have hit 739 mph in mid-December 1979. For the first time in land speed history, the car was travelling so fast that the team needed a satellite to time the run correctly. The team later claimed it had broken the sound barrier, although others questioned this, on the basis that they'd not heard a sonic boom. For regulatory reasons, the speed was not recognized by the FIA, and so Gary Gabelich remained the official top dog for the next thirteen years. The ratified speed records from the early 1960s until the 1970 mark of 622.407 mph had increased by a staggering 219 mph, a frankly astonishing increment of 54 per cent.

Like many of his fellow speed merchants, Gabelich lived to go fast and was still

chasing records in the early 1980s. Unfortunately, after a terrible drag race accident that nearly tore off his left hand and badly broke his left leg, Gabelich was preparing for a new land speed record attempt when he died in a motorbike accident on the road in 1984.

It seems that no matter how many tragedies litter the land speed playing fields, there are always new competitors willing to put everything on the line for that top speed mark. It is a very specific type of personality that jumps into these land-based missiles - it is not hyperbole to suggest that, when they strap themselves in, these remarkable individuals know that in a few minutes' time they will potentially either be the new land speed record holder ... or dead.

*Aerial view of the wreckage of Art Arfons' Green Monster, after crashing during an attempt to break the world land speed record at Bonneville Speedway in 1966.*

# Chapter 12

# Speed
## Exotica

*Speed now illuminates reality whereas light once gave objects of the world their shape.*

French theorist and philosopher Paul Virilio

While Breedlove, Arfons, Green et al were hurtling across the earth's crust at ludicrous speeds, back in the relatively slower world of high-performance sports cars, both sides of the Atlantic were developing and evolving the wider public's road-going experience of speed, and coming at that challenge from very different positions.

While the Ton Up Boys and hot rod racers of the 1950s were taking the experience of speed off the race track and salt lakes into the roads of everyday towns, democratizing the sensation for the masses, the more elite vehicles of the automotive world were notably absent from the narrative. As discussed earlier, the decade of the first teenagers, soundtracked by rock 'n' roll, was fairly barren for the high-performance motor car, with a fashion for sensible, frugal family cars with only a few notable exceptions.

*The Lamborghini Countach remains one of the most striking and extravagant of all supercars.*

However, back in the original hotbed of automotive speed, continental Europe, the motoring industry was hardly inactive. The European performance car fraternity began to launch their own very special contribution to the history of speed. Through a combination of art, science and a very European flair, the road-going experience of speed was about to undergo a revolution. Of course, cars had been getting progressively quicker ever since the 1885 Motorwagen, but the 1960s saw a condensed acceleration of this process with the advent - and savage evolution - of the modern supercar.

The first signs of this sea-change had come back in 1954 with the launch of the Mercedes 300SL, known as the Gullwing. During the Second World War, the factories of Daimler-Benz had been razed to the ground in the Allied bombing raids, so this famous supercar was born out of economic necessity from the loins of the all-conquering Silver Arrows race team, essentially being a road-going version of its Le Mans winning predecessor, combined with DNA from the hugely successful Mercedes 300 Sedan. The car boasted a number of high-tech developments such as a space-frame chassis (which created the need for the futuristic gullwing doors), independent suspension and the first use of direct fuel injection in a road car. The Gullwing wasn't just beautiful – it was also touted on its release as the fastest production car in the world, capable of hitting 160 mph in an era when 100 mph was

*The revolutionary Mercedes 300SL Gullwing was the fastest car in the world on its launch and immediately made all its rival cars look old-fashioned.*

The Gullwing's famous eponymous doors were actually a design necessity, created to accommodate the high sills of its pioneering space-frame chassis.

considered swift. A contemporary review said the 300SL 'alarms the populace by its rapid acceleration'. After the Gullwing, this claim to be the fastest production car in the world became a ritual for car manufacturers that would become a fixture of almost every forthcoming supercar launch. Speed, it seems, will always matter when it comes to selling.

The next European speed milestone in terms of road cars is the seminal Lamborghini Miura, the first mid-engined performance car and one almost universally regarded as the first modern supercar. Taking the mid-engine layout from motorsports, thus creating a lower centre of gravity and sleeker looks for road cars, this Italian revelation stunned the world of speed on its launch at the Turin Motor Show in 1965. Most remarkably, the car's origins lie in tractors, air-conditioning units and gas heaters - all trades where the marque's founder, Ferrucio Lamborghini, had made his fortune. Legend has it that he was tired of the poor clutch control on the Ferrari he had bought so, living near to Enzo Ferrari, he called in on the Modena factory of the prancing horse to resolve the issue. However, Enzo was, as rumour had it, far from welcoming and sent

*The first mid-engined modern supercar – the Lamborghini Miura, an Italian masterpiece.*

Ferrucio packing, deriding his tractors and his engineering know-how. So Ferrucio, a former Italian RAF mechanic and the son of viticulturists, simply decided to build his own supercar and, in so doing, created the raging bull marque.

After an early 2+2 car, Ferrucio dazzled the world with a Miura rolling chassis at the Turin Motor Show - so stunning and revolutionary was the car that he was besieged with orders on the spot. Its top speed was around 170 mph, which by modern standards is relatively modest - but in the context of the 1960s the car was ballistic. Overnight, cars such as the Ferrari 365GTB/4 looked out of date. The Miura's design motifs around a bull's physiology and the car's sleek, predatory lines have all become markers of supercar legend, but in terms of speed, the Miura upped the ante massively - because from here on manufacturers knew there was big money to be made in the genre. Remember, Lamborghini were not using the

Miura to sell cheaper, entry-level models. This was a supercar for the sake of being a supercar. Fast for the sake of going fast.

What the Miura also did for speed was thrust the supercar into the modern lexicon – famously featured in the opening scene of the Michael Caine classic *The Italian Job*, the car came to epitomize style and speed as a desirable marriage in modern society. In a decade when 'peace and love' was joined by growing anti-capitalist undercurrents, the relevance of supercars might have been cast into doubt, but instead the Miura cemented the continuing appeal of a car that was too fast for any standard speed limit and too expensive for all but the very wealthy (itself in direct contrast to the mass-market democratization of speed during the previous decade). Indirectly, the success of this Italian car also incited other manufacturers' pursuit of speed because, suitably piqued and commercially envious, all Lamborghini's competitors upped their game. The Miura had effectively started the modern supercar arms race to be the fastest road car on earth.

By the 1970s, family cars and new 4×4s with luggage space and safety features were all the vogue, yet this most peculiar of modern engineering manifestations - the exorbitantly priced supercar - was entering its first golden era, an affirmation of the collective and ongoing social fascination with speed. This was all the more counter-intuitive because of the two crippling oil crises in this decade, ever stricter emissions

*The upward flick on the Miura's doors mimic a bull's horns.*

On the license plate: GHL 25

regulations and lowered speed limits such as a mere 55 mph in the USA. Further, the genealogical link between racing cars and road-going vehicles was now almost entirely separated, with the days long since gone of racing cars simply being tuned versions of road models. There was now effectively no remaining symbiosis between the two previous bedfellows at all.

The 1970s would prove to be the decade of futuristic supercars, with manufacturers producing cars that might look more at home in a sci-fi movie. Most supercars from this decade look fast standing still. Paradoxically, these futuristic wedge-shaped supercars were not actually very aerodynamic, so to some degree this was a fake, superficial representation of speed. However, there were some stand-out cars that took speed on to the next level. Lamborghini did it again in 1974 with the legendary Countach,

*Reversing in a Countach was so difficult due to poor visibility that owners had to open the scissor door, sit on the sill and peer backwards out of the cabin.*

named after a (non-obscene) expletive in the Piedmontese dialect of Italian that is uttered when a man sees a very beautiful woman. Again it looked astonishing (still does), and again it was the fastest car in the world when launched. A theme was recurring …

Similar speed machines such as the Lotus Esprit, BMW M1 and De Tomaso Pantera ramped up the supercar arms race. This was all despite the majority of these cars being absurdly impractical, with heavy clutches, virtually zero rear visibility and often poor build quality. The admiring general public seemed not to care: they couldn't afford them, wouldn't enjoy driving them but still put posters of them up in millions of homes around the world.

# Chapter 13

# Muscle
# Mania

*Car shows such as* The Dukes of Hazzard *put the muscle car – and, by definition, speed – in the living rooms of millions of people worldwide.*

*America is all about speed. Hot, nasty, badass speed.*

Will Ferrell

Across in the USA, an external factor showed its hand during the 1960s and 1970s that brought the notion of going fast to new levels of universality, expanding massively on the democratization of speed first stoked by the Ton Up Boys and hot rod racers of previous years.

Those two decades saw speed impacted massively by a cultural phenomenon that would indelibly alter the history of going fast - television. Although television

had been invented decades earlier, the widespread adoption of TV sets in most homes did not become a reality until the 1950s, and more in the 1960s. In turn, what this did was put speed into the living rooms of millions of people worldwide. During the glory days of the land speed monsters in the 1920s, the drivers were huge celebrities, but this was a status bestowed on them by the spectators who had witnessed their daring feats in person, as well as the

newspapers and newsreel showings at cinemas. The birth of the modern TV culture in the home suddenly put speed alongside advertisements for kitchen appliances and tinned food, in a sense making high speed an everyday commodity.

The twin behemoths of television and the movies championed this glamorization of speed. The first US show to highlight a star car was *Route 66* in 1960. Thereafter, countless films featured famous car chases - *Bullitt*, the original *Gone in 60 Seconds*, *The French Connection*, *Vanishing Point* and, arguably most notably of all, *The Italian Job*. Television took these speed vignettes even further, particularly in the 1970s, when car-themed shows and films were huge across the globe - perhaps most famously, *Smokey and the Bandit* and *The Dukes of Hazzard*. Eating a TV dinner that had been cooked in a microwave oven and washed by a dishwasher afterwards was a very modern indulgence, topped off with an inordinate choice of films or TV shows where cars were driven on public roads at breakneck speeds. Critics argued that the sheer volume of wild car chases on television and in the movies effectively normalized dangerous driving, exposing generations of kids to apparently acceptable illegal speeding in the comfort of their own

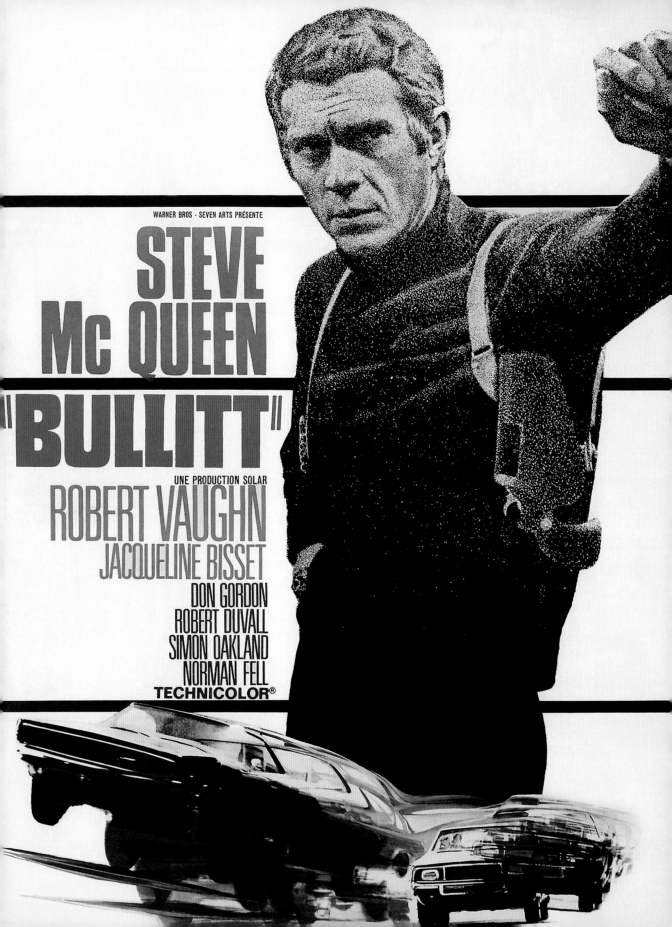

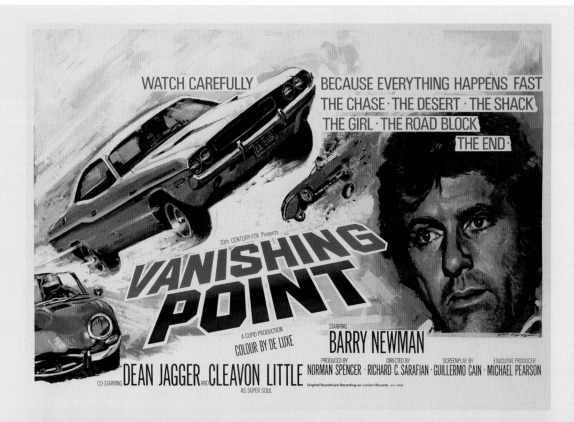

# MICHAEL CAINE
# NOËL COWARD

• 1969 - 1999 •
**RELEASED**
• AFTER 30 YEARS •

# THE

THIS IS THE SELF PRESERVATION SOCIETY

# ITALIAN
# JOB

PG

"the Michael Cain
crime corker is bar
a classi
not to be miss

homes. This seemed not to matter to the millions of fans of these hugely popular shows and films.

This visual accessibility and prevalence of speed within the home coincided with road-going cars becoming ever faster, to the degree that hot rods and street racers could increasingly be matched by sports cars purchased straight from mainstream dealerships. A classic example of how the evolution of road-going cars has changed the history of speed immeasurably in this way is the American muscle car, a genre that indelibly implanted everyday speed into the lives of millions of people.

At the time, the USA was not renowned for building supercars. While the Americans dominated land speed during these years, in terms of road-going speed, the USA was somewhat behind the continental European game. Instead, North America was consistently the biggest market for imports of European brands such as Ferrari, Porsche and Lamborghini. Somewhat affronted by this overseas success, the USA decided to create its own vehicles that approached speed from a much less nimble but far more brutal stance: muscle cars.

This genre of speed machine is generally deemed to be a mid-sized American vehicle with savage acceleration and a large displacement front engine (typically V8s), powered by rear-wheel drive. In terms of speed, muscle was all about acceleration – with a speed limit of 70 mph imposed in most US states by the end of the 1960s, top speeds were not seen as particularly relevant to muscle car enthusiasts. The quarter mile sprint was the standard, with a time of less than 16 seconds being the preferred performance. Sometimes, in chasing these faster sprint times, manufacturers would undertake unofficial tests, with rumours of some car designers secretly working with illegal street racers to develop new parts. Muscle cars were not necessarily refined. Build quality was often poor. Detractors said they were fast in a straight line but couldn't go round corners. Brakes often barely worked at all. This didn't matter to a country riddled with huge long, straight roads and cheap gas on every corner.

Muscle cars were usually allied quite closely to an equivalent standard model. The idea of putting a massive engine in a standard-bodied car was itself a throwback to hot rods of the pre-war era. 1960s muscle cars were often relatively modest in looks, partly appealing to those drivers who might not want to attract the attention of law enforcement. That said, there was a tendency for these models to bulge in certain areas of the bodywork, as if literally straining the muscles to keep the power underneath in check. The visual similarity to more standard spec cars was quite deliberate and all part of the commercial *raison d'être* for the existence of muscle cars - to help manufacturers sell greater volumes of their more affordable, lower-performance models. Notably, these muscular machines were not actually marketed as muscle cars at the time. Also, actual sales volumes were quite modest, with many high-profile models only selling in the hundreds; but the trickle-down effect on sales of cheaper models - termed the halo effect in the motor trade - was enormous.

The genealogy of muscle cars is hotly debated. Culturally, early hot rods and the National Association for Stock Car Auto Racing (NASCAR) had certainly created a love for fast cars in the USA's social underbelly. A number of early variants such as the Rambler Rebel, Max Wedge Mopars and Chrysler 300 can lay claim to helping start the muscle car movement, but in terms of mainstream profile, there is a general acceptance that the Pontiac GTO was one of the very first muscle cars to create a mass-market impact. Pontiac had enjoyed success on the drag strip and in NASCAR, and then a very famous *Car and Driver* magazine cover feature showed the Pontiac GTO racing a beautiful red Ferrari GTO. Nicknamed 'the Goat', the Pontiac GTO broke all manner of sales records. Pontiac had hoped to sell 5000 GTOs in the first year; they sold 32,000. Ford enjoyed similar success with their Mustang, particularly when Steve McQueen appeared in one in the 1968 movie *Bullitt*, to this day considered by many to be the coolest movie car (and car chase) of all time. After that, the popularity of the genre exploded: there are too many muscle cars to mention here, but classics include the Dodge Challenger, the Roadrunner, the Dodge Charger, the Pontiac Firebird, a Chevy Camaro and a 1968 Plymouth Hemi.

The social backdrop to this mass American adoption of affordable speed was the era of the Great Society trumpeted by President Lyndon Johnson. Jumping into a daily driver that was fast and exciting, and often seen being driven by enigmatic TV and movie stars, made the muscle car a crucial part of this American ideal. The 1960s, as well as the earlier years of the 1970s, was the golden era of the genre. Seen on every American street, muscle cars became TV and movie stars themselves, which in turn led to merchandise, toys, clothing and utensils; in fact almost any facet of contemporary American life might have a fast muscle car emblazoned on it. This omnipresence in US popular culture was not just a gimmick seen on television – unlike their expensive European supercar counterparts, muscle cars opened up speed to millions of everyday people because they were relatively affordable, making them a massive part of US motoring life.

However, as has so often been the case, the history of speed remained at the liberty of social change. The 1970s would sound the death knell of the muscle car, with stricter emissions regulations, higher insurance premiums and oil crises during the mid-1970s that began to chip away at muscle cars' popularity, such that, by the later years of the decade, the genre was all but extinct. Even so, the impact of the muscle car on the history of speed is undeniable.

Both the supercar and muscle car genre changed the history of speed massively – the former marking a return to extreme glamour and exclusivity around the notion of going fast, while the latter made speed a daily and affordable experience for the masses. By the end of the 1970s, speed – whether aspirational or actual – was a constant part of daily life.

*One of the most iconic of all muscle cars, the Pontiac GTO. Although often perceived as a US-only phenomenon, muscle cars are in fact an international breed, with the cultural impact of these machines spread around the globe, helped massively by the success of internationally successful US films and TV shows.*

# Chapter 14

# Coffins on Water

*You don't drive the boat, you wear it.*

Ken Warby, current outright water speed record holder, a mark that remains undefeated since 1978

Although this book is largely a study of wheel-based speed merchants, with an admitted bias towards vehicles classified as cars, the 1970s brings with it a necessary diversion into the world of the water speed record. In previous decades, land and water speed champions frequently crossed over the two disciplines, but the water speed record was always considered far more dangerous. In short, it is one of the most dangerous speed pursuits any person can chase. The current unlimited water speed record stands at 317.596 mph, set by Australian Ken Warby. Since that astonishing world best mark, two attempts have been made to break his landmark figure - by Lee Taylor and Craig Arfons - both of which ended in the death of the competitor. It isn't just the outright top speed figure that is extremely dangerous on water - during the writing of this book, three people were killed in an attempt to break the offshore speed record, including Italian ten-times world champion Fabio Buzzi (who was also the diesel boat record holder). The water record is regarded as so dangerous that author Bill Tuckey even wrote a book about

current record holder Ken Warby entitled *The World's Fastest Coffin on Water*.

Part of the challenge is that water as a dynamic medium is 800 times denser than air. To hit the top speeds, boats have to raise themselves out of the water, known as hydroplaning, but this leaves only a few square inches of the vessel actually touching the water. Stability is everything yet is also highly unpredictable. The forces at work on water speed boats are shocking. As explained by *Wire* magazine's Carl Hoffman in a 2003 article named 'Cheating Death', for every doubling of speed, the aerodynamic lift is quadrupled - meaning that many boats take off altogether when they lose their delicate stability. Too much downforce in the design pushes the boat into the water too savagely at speed, causing it to be popped into the air; too little drag and the boat takes off. 'Either way,' says Hoffman, 'you are dead.'

*American Gar Wood, boat builder, racer and water speed record holder, the first person to exceed 100 mph on water.*

Even if the boat is engineered to perfection, the very nature of water introduces a number of unpredictable and potentially catastrophic peripheral elements. For example, an unexpected wake in the water cannot be avoided with certainty, yet can cause instant tragedy. If an aeroplane tilts a few inches to the left or right, that can be corrected without incident; if a water speed boat does the same, a potentially fatal accident will likely be unavoidable.

Water speed records have existed almost as long as land speed marks. Steam-powered, propeller-driven boats were the first machines used, with Nathanael Herreshoff's 26.2 mph in 1885 being widely recognized as the first verified record. Many pioneering engineers made attempts, even including Alexander Graham Bell, the inventor of the telephone. One early star was American inventor Garfield 'Gar' Wood, who set new records on numerous occasions with boats such as Miss America, including being, in 1931, the first person to exceed 100 mph on water (102.256 mph). Wood vied with his contemporary Kaye Don in the early 1930s

until (as mentioned earlier) the Englishman Malcolm Campbell entered the fray with his Bluebirds (setting four records in two years). Like land speed, the water record often veered into national rivalry, largely at this point between the USA and Britain.

As with land speed, the Second World War enforced a hiatus, but when water speed record attempts returned the stakes were similarly raised. Stanley Sayres was first off, with his Slo-Mo-Shun IV setting a new mark of 160.323 mph in 1950. Disaster struck again in 1952 when English speed king John Cobb died on Loch Ness, as previously mentioned; two years later, Italian textile magnate Mario Verga also lost his life attempting the record, this time on Lake Iseo in northern Italy. Both tragedies underlined just how exceptionally dangerous this most dramatic and precarious speed challenge remained.

In 1955, Donald Campbell continued his family legacy with a string of water speed records, starting with the first ever 200 mph run (202.32 mph), followed by a series of increments varying from 9 to 16 mph, before being beaten by the USA's Lee Taylor in his 285.22 mph Hustler, which set that mark six months after Campbell's tragic early demise on Coniston Water. (At the time of writing, Campbell nevertheless remains the most prolific water speed record breaker of all time.) For his part, Taylor soon had his own brush with death – during a test run on Lake Havasu in 1964, he was unable to shut down his jet engine and hurtled into the side of the lake at over 100 mph, being critically injured in the process. Like so many speed mavericks before him, Taylor recovered, rebuilt his boat and proceeded to smash the record three years later (but, tragically, he would drown during an attempt at the record in 1980).

By 1977, the first Australian water speed record holder had arrived, in the shape of one of speed's all-time greatest mavericks, Ken Warby. In that year, he set a new record of 288.60 mph, but it was what he did the following year that remains the subject of true speed legend. As mentioned, at the time of writing, some four decades later, the existing water speed record *still* belongs to Warby, who was also the first person outside of North America, Ireland or Britain to hold the crown. In October 1978, he took his craft, the Spirit of Australia, to a mind-boggling speed of 317.596 mph on Blowering Dam. This was the average velocity; his peak speed was actually significantly higher, at 345 mph. He remains the only human to ever exceed 300 mph on water and survive.

Warby's own story is more remarkable than any fiction. Working for Makita, selling power tools and rock drilling equipment in the 1970s, Ken had a fascination with speed and water and so, as only this particular breed of speed freaks are wont to do, he decided to design the hull at home. When he was a 14-year-old, boat-obsessed lad, he had built his first craft in his garden - so now, he figured, that was exactly what he would do again. That childhood passion had morphed into a successful boat racing career in the 1960s (including state and national championships), so he was by no means a newcomer to speed on water, but nonetheless funds were short.

A former engineer and soldier in the 14th Field Squadron Royal Australian Engineers, Ken drew up the designs on his kitchen table in 1970 and two years later began construction in his backyard. Trickily, this meant he had to work around daylight hours and only in good weather. He had very little money, so bought parts as and when he could afford to - at one point he was only able to purchase a piece of plywood with his funds. He only used three power tools - a drill, a circular saw and a belt sander; everything else was made with old-school hand tools.

The entire craft was created with a modest $10,000 budget. Working with two military personnel friends, Warby bought three RAAF surplus Westinghouse J-34 jet engines at a low-key auction for $269 in total. One power plant did not even function, but a lengthy rebuild eventually corrected that.

Warby began testing before the boat was fully completed, because his restricted budget simply did not allow for extravagant purchases such as cowlings, air intakes and tailplanes. Nonetheless, his genius and bravery were sufficient to take this craft to a new Australian water speed record. However, his sights were set much higher, so he began to research a longer stretch of water that would accommodate the record-breaking speeds he had in mind. All this despite the fact he had never previously travelled faster than 87 mph. That was not about to stop Ken.

With the financial demands of the project, Ken was forced to quit his job, to generate sponsorship and income for the build. He took the boat around Shell service stations all over Australia and even took up oil painting for money, selling his art at shopping centres to raise more funding. Sponsors included his local store, Fosseys.

However, this was no Heath Robinson amateur dramatics – Warby had a deep understanding of water dynamics and spent three weeks just thinking about the rudder alone. Ken also teamed up with a number of experts for his speed bid, including Tom Fink, a professor at NSW University who had worked on the aero and testing for Donald Campbell's Bluebird K7. He also recruited various RAAF experts, who helped him in their free time. Finally, in mid-1977, Ken took his craft – the Spirit of Australia – to a record-breaking 288.60 mph on the Blowering Dam, but he was far from satisfied. Modifications were implemented (again all self-funded)

and in 1978 he went to the same stretch of water again to push the boundaries even more. The night before the record attempt, Fink and Ken spoke at length on the telephone about the rudder, and with the use of a friend's blowtorch in a local farmer's shed, that part was shortened by 65 mm.

On 8 October that year, Ken Warby piloted his wooden, jet-powered boat to an average of 317.596 mph on a still day at the Dam, simultaneously smashing the legendary

*Ken Warby setting the existing water speed record of 317.596 mph in 1978.*

300 mph and 310 mph barriers. That speed represents 0.62 miles every 7 seconds. The water remained open to recreational fishermen and sightseers during the attempt.

As mentioned, his astonishing high speed mark has since proved fatal to anyone trying to emulate his achievement. This incredibly romantic, some would say charming, tale actually hides an acutely perceptive brain, and in fact the reasons for the project's historical success are rooted in sound engineering. Ken never tested the craft beyond what he felt were its limitations at the time; he built up the boat and the target speeds gradually, honing and modifying only after actual, real-world experience; he used the basic design principles he had learnt as an engineer and applied them in intelligent and beautifully simple ways; and whenever a problem was encountered, he would make no further speed runs until that issue was resolved. From start to finish, the project took eight years; a sagely slow way to travel exceedingly fast.

One final note: Ken did not fit a seatbelt as he felt his design was comprehensive and the solid, well-considered design would prevail. Over forty years later, with his record still intact, he remains the only person ever to design, build and drive a boat to an outright, unlimited world water speed record. So he was right.

*A brilliant engineer and designer, Warby remains the only person ever to exceed 300 mph on water and survive.*

# Chapter 15

# Trickle Down

*Faster, faster, until the thrill of speed overcomes the fear of death.*
Author Hunter S. Thompson

In any study of the history of speed, racing cars are inevitably involved - the stories of the Bentley Boys, the Bugatti Queen and their ilk will always be of interest to those fascinated by speed. However, many forms of motor racing are not actually about the pursuit of speed (which is why they do not feature heavily in this book). Of course, there are many elements of motor sport that are focused on going quickly, but the simple fact is that a racing driver will want to stand on the top of the podium *above all else*. They want to be first, not fastest. Some motorsports - such as Formula 1 with a new rule in 2019 - acknowledge the fastest lap of a race with extra points, but that does not motivate any winning racer. It has absolutely never been a given that the fastest race car will necessarily always win, because there are so many other factors to consider - tyre use, fuel load, cornering ability, pit stop strategy, pit stop speed - the list is almost endless.

Indeed, many racers win more trophies by being strategically astute, even racing defensively against charging opponents, using brinksmanship in braking, deliberately going slower or nursing their engine or brakes. Formula 1 operations manager Neil Waterman takes it further:

*In fact, there is a chance that if they go too fast they won't even finish the race. Using Le Mans*

as an example: at the end of the Mulsanne straight, you'd brake from 240 mph and come down to 100 mph for the corner, and you'd do that in 1.1 seconds. So actually, for many race drivers, deceleration is more pivotal and indeed dramatic than speed or acceleration.

The thrill is in the win, nothing else; first is all that counts, and everyone else loses. Former racing driver John Morrison, who has won multiple international races including Daytona, has this to say:

*Speed itself is absolutely irrelevant to a race driver. To me, it was all about winning and whatever you had to do to get there. I am sure it is the same for any performance athlete. The only thing that matters is the time, not the speed in comparison with others. I knew doing 200 mph down the Mulsanne in the wet at night was a bit hairy, but anything over 130 mph was fast anyway. But essentially we were only doing it to compete. You could have said to me, 'Do you realize you are doing 230 mph?' I wouldn't have known or cared. Speed really didn't matter.*

This is not, of course, to say that elite racing cars are not quick - far from it. Neil Waterman continues:

*A modern F1 car can accelerate to 60 mph in less than 2 seconds, generate more G-Force than the Space Shuttle launch, and hit over 200 mph in qualifying trim. However, these remarkable cars are rarely unleashed to their full speed potential. F1 cars are geared for each circuit, so their potential top speed is never actually achieved. However, speeds of over 230 mph in the 1990s and 2000s have been reached at the old circuit in Hockenheim, which boasts a very long straight, and similar speeds have been recorded at Monza. It is also worth remembering that Formula 1 deliberately clipped speeds in the 1970s, when cars were becoming so rapid - even in cornering with the revolutionary use of ground effect - that driver fatalities and injuries were almost out of control. So F1 is, to be fair, a sport that could go much, much faster.*

But also bear in mind that the 1930s Mercedes and Auto-Unions F1 cars were also capable of

An F1 car running at Bonneville – Formula 1 prides itself on pushing speed boundaries: at the 2019 German Grand Prix, Red Bull Racing changed all four tyres on Max Verstappen's race car and sent him back out in 1.88 seconds – the fastest pit stop ever.

*200+ mph. Formula 1 has on occasion tested these top speed limits, such as when Honda set an official FIA sanctioned land speed record on the 2006 Bonneville Salt Flats and reached 397 kph (246 mph).*

However, despite Waterman's highly pertinent points about motor racing speeds, the simple fact is that a standard issue 2019 Bugatti Chiron has a top speed limit that is in the region of 50 mph quicker than most Formula 1 cars. So, no, many levels of motorsport are not a major factor in the history of speed, in that sense.

Where motorsport *has* altered speed's evolution is in the influence these cars have on everyday vehicles. Top level motorsport has developed and later bequeathed many technological innovations, as Waterman explains:

*The development of various 'active car systems' (ultimately banned in F1) has filtered down into supercars, but in a wider sense motorsport has bequeathed traction control, semi-automatic gear changes, active suspension, active aerodynamics. In addition, ever-improving safety features such as crash or impact structures and headrest technology also led to improvements in the design of child car seats. In the twenty-first century, braking systems and brake materials, heat rejection efficiency (cooling), oils, fuels and lubricants, hybrid powertrain systems, energy storage, composite materials (light and strong), even styling owes a lot to the development of motorsport through the use of CFD (Computational Fluid Dynamics), widely used in top-level racing design to optimize aerodynamic efficiency. Motor racing circuits' safety barrier technology has even filtered across onto public roads.*

These innovations have led to quicker, safer, more robust and generally higher-performing road cars. In the first instance, motorsport innovation influences speed by affecting the development of supercars, and certainly during the last quarter of the twentieth century the advances made in this glamorous genre of speed machine are remarkable.

As worries about emissions and safety grew, the supercar speed arms race, rather than petering out, really ramped up towards the end of the 1970s and into the 1980s when, like their land speed cousins before them, supercar manufacturers began to eye the 200 mph barrier enviously. Land speed cars had hit this mark way back in 1927 with Sir Henry Segrave at the wheel – an absolute age in speed terms – but the time was approaching when a sufficiently big cheque book could buy anyone the ability to travel at this mind-boggling speed, the equivalent of a football pitch in 1 second.

In the 1980s, manufacturers of high-performance cars were spurred on by a consumerist global economy that championed the Yuppie and conspicuous consumption. Supercars were suddenly very much in vogue: the bigger, louder and - crucially here - faster, the better. By this point, the supercar was a perennial element of modern culture; the full force of galloping and ever-evolving new technology, a booming consumerist society and increasingly better roads meant that fast cars found themselves entering a new era.

Previously the road speed kings had been Ferrari and Lamborghini, battling away with precious new cars aimed at outdoing each other. However, in 1985, the Stuttgart-based, racing-inspired manufacturer Porsche entered the fray with their technologically advanced 959. Intended to be the extreme iteration of their famous Porsche 911 sports car, the 959 would become famous for a host of technological advances that made daily high speed a more controlled and measured experience. The 959 was actually conceived with the deadly Group B rally series in mind, a formula that had few limits on power in its race cars but was eventually abandoned due to a number of horrific accidents and fatalities. Porsche had intended to use the car to meet the 200 units the FIA required to homologate Group B entrants, but by the time the series was stopped, the German manufacturer had invested heavily in the car's development and so continued with its full evolution as a road car. Consequently, the Porsche 959 was quite simply the most technologically advanced car ever seen: computer-controlled four-wheel drive; torque vectoring allowing power to move between front and rear wheels depending

*The Porsche 959 was a technological tour de force and took road-going supercar science – and speeds – to new heights.*

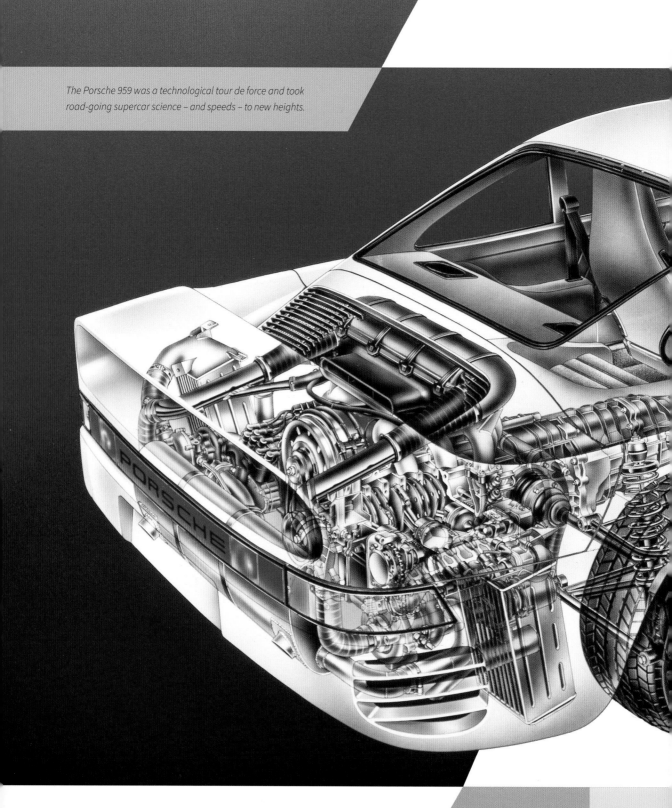

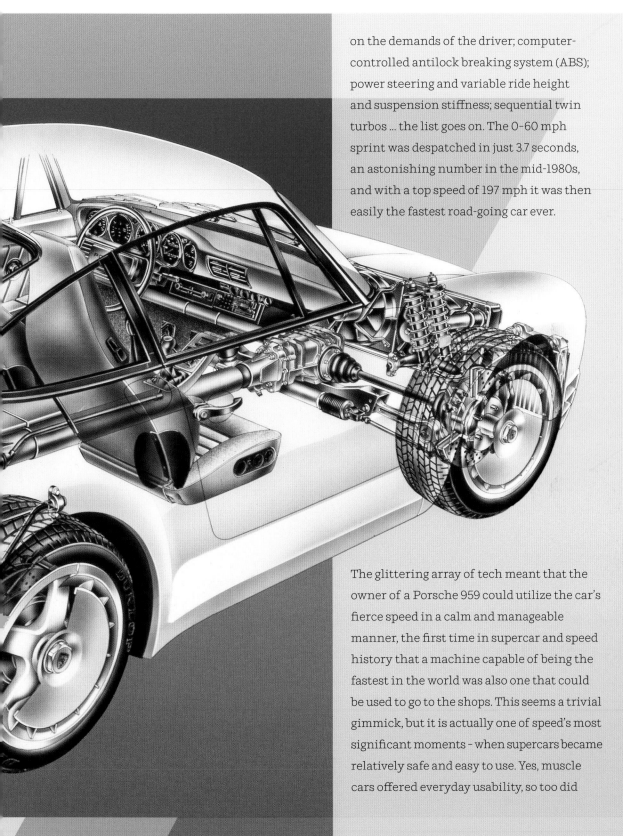

on the demands of the driver; computer-controlled antilock breaking system (ABS); power steering and variable ride height and suspension stiffness; sequential twin turbos ... the list goes on. The 0-60 mph sprint was despatched in just 3.7 seconds, an astonishing number in the mid-1980s, and with a top speed of 197 mph it was then easily the fastest road-going car ever.

The glittering array of tech meant that the owner of a Porsche 959 could utilize the car's fierce speed in a calm and manageable manner, the first time in supercar and speed history that a machine capable of being the fastest in the world was also one that could be used to go to the shops. This seems a trivial gimmick, but it is actually one of speed's most significant moments – when supercars became relatively safe and easy to use. Yes, muscle cars offered everyday usability, so too did

certain GT cars – but this was the fastest car in the world equally at home cruising gently along a high street. The normalization of extreme speed continued apace.

With delightful Italian hubris, Ferrari responded to the easy-to-use Porsche 959 with a rival car that was brutally fast and savage, spectacularly aggressive and – monumentally – capable of hitting 200 mph: the twin-turbo F40, the very first road car ever to hit that magical double ton. The increasing use of motor-racing composite materials such as kevlar and carbon fibre in supercars meant that vehicles such as the Ferrari 288GTO and F40 could produce race-car speeds and handling, albeit at an eye-watering cost. The 478 hp, 2.9 litre V8 F40 had been designed to celebrate the fortieth anniversary of the famous marque and heralded a number of

144

What these modern supercars were doing was focusing society on top speeds that were both illegal and entirely unachievable in practical terms. After the F40 pierced 200 mph for the first time in a road car, the world of supercars became obsessed with top speed for the next thirty years. Of course, the all-important 0-60 mph sprint was still crucial and always mentioned in any sales brochures or at the countless swanky car show launches, but it was top speed that was the main badge of honour. Bugatti's relaunched brand produced the EB110 to enter the fray in 1991. The Jaguar XJ220 was next up, capable of the speed its name suggested (like the XK120 before it). Even though the British marque's purists did not like the relatively agricultural V6 engine, it was still capable of four times the US speed limit. Then came a vehicle that redefined supercars but which also - by winning Le Mans at the first attempt - turned the clock back to the golden days of speed: Gordon Murray's legendary F1. His three-seater car

advances, albeit couched in a savagely raw car (no ABS, no airbags, no brake servo, no power steering), but the main headline was always going to be the top speed of 202 mph. The speedo offered a tempting 225 mph and a tuned F40 was clocked hitting 226 mph on the Bonneville Salt Flats, a fitting tribute to the land speed ancestors slamming across those dry lake beds decades earlier.

obliterated all competition in the world of supercars, being the most expensive ever (£635,000), quickest to 60 mph and to 100 mph and then, inevitably, breaking the speed record for a production car when it hit 240.1 mph in 1998, with Le Mans winner Andy Wallace at the wheel.

There is an important caveat to the modern supercar's impact on the history of speed – for all but a very tiny minority, these supercars remained a vicarious experience of speed. A bedroom poster for millions of children, maybe, but rarely a feasible car in the garage. However, what this breed of elite speed machines did do was generate massive cultural interest that would eventually manifest itself in a far more widespread experience of speed. While the person in the street admired the Ferrari F40 or McLaren F1 from afar, from the 1980s onwards there was an increasing accumulation of seemingly normal cars that actually offered supercar performance. Significantly for the history of speed, the last two decades of the twentieth century would see everyday cars becoming ever faster in a seismic shift in the availability of these newly savage speeds. It was no longer just rally kings and

European supercars that offered extreme speed and race-inspired technology. By the late 1970s and early 1980s, mass market manufacturers such as Ford, Peugeot and Audi were realizing that there was profit in affordable speed. Cars such as the Ford Sierra Cosworth and Escort XR3i, Peugeot's 205 GTi 1.9 and, of course, the VW Golf GTi, were all normal cars capable of supercar performance. This became the era of the hot hatch, when smaller, lighter cars were being packed with powerful engines, sports handling and performance capabilities. Although there are early examples of the genre as far back as BMW's 1971 2000 Ti Touring and the Autobianchi A112, the Golf GTi is seen as the watershed car, followed by others from Ford, Peugeot, Renault and so on, offering affordable agility, fun and, above all, speed. These cars were generally the most expensive model in the range, but even so they were still far cheaper than contemporary supercars.

There are a number of technological breakthroughs that enabled this dissemination of speed across the more mainstream motoring sector. Certainly the four-wheel drive system pioneered in the all-conquering Audi Quattro rally champion car would filter down and make handling and the everyday use of speed far easier and safer, as would the growing use of computers for traction control. The advent of the turbo was another mechanism for pure speed improvement – the BMW 2002 had trialled this technology initially, but it was the Porsche 911-930 Turbo that took all the glory. Taking exhaust gases and slamming them through a turbo to create a power boost that could be savage, the 911 Turbo was a crude and brutal piece of kit. The problem was turbo lag: after the accelerator was floored the power boost might arrive several seconds later, at a seemingly indeterminate point, so a driver could get a huge boost in speed just as they turned into a corner. Consequently, finding an original 911 Turbo that hasn't suffered significant accident damage has become a very rare feat.

While the gap in like-for-like performance between supercars and fast everyday cars was decreasing through the 1980s onwards, this proliferation of ever quicker normal cars also continued an engineering evolution that had started back in the 1940s. For example, the first 1940s iterations of the people's car, the Volkswagen Beetle, in standard trim, could accelerate to 60 mph in around 25 seconds; at the time of writing, the equivalent entry-level family car, the VW T-Cross, can do the same sprint in just 10 seconds. If you stretched your budget and bought the fastest VW Golf R, you'd get to the 60 mph in just 4.6 seconds. That's just half a second slower than a contemporary Porsche 911 Carrera 4S. A 2015 BMW 1 Series 120d may be a diesel-engined car but it is quicker than Ferrari's 1977 308GTB … while doing as much as 65 mpg. These fast, everyday cars are proof positive that the general infection of speed into mass market cars – and everyday life – can be found in all price points of the car industry.

This theme will be revisited in the later chapter, 'A Few Facts about Speed', but suffice to say, the proliferation of super-quick road-going cars that were affordable to almost anyone in the 1980s ensured that genuinely rapid speeds were no longer a rarity on public roads or something for the well-heeled elite. This was mass-produced speed. From the 1980s onwards, if you could get credit, you could go fast.

# Chapter 16

# The Psychology of
# Speed

*The person travelling at the fastest pace does not always arrive at their destination first.*

Author and motivational speaker Rasheed Ogunlaru

In the modern era of speed, there is a massive and problematic paradox at the heart of road-going automobiles: anyone with enough cash (or credit) can buy a car capable of achieving speeds that a few decades previously would have registered as a land speed record. Even away from the world of supercars, modern cars routinely offer top speeds over 150 mph and extremely rapid acceleration. The problem is that, while the technology and affordability of speed has taken huge leaps forward year after year since the Second World War, the human beings driving these machines are essentially exactly the same. The human brain and body has not evolved to the same degree as speed in such a short space of time. This implies that modern drivers are not necessarily as well equipped or capable as their advanced cars of tolerating or handling higher speeds, which prompts the question: what exactly happens physically and mentally when we travel in a vehicle at high speed?

Firstly, the biology of speed creates a definite physical chain of events in the brain and body, swamping the individual with a heady cocktail of chemicals and hormones. The most obvious one is a rush of adrenaline (also known as epinephrine), a hormone and neurotransmitter that is inextricably linked to the human experience of speed. Under stress - or exhilaration - this powerful natural chemical is sent coursing around the body as part of the ingrained fight or flight response (known clinically as an acute stress response). A shot of adrenaline leads to raised blood pressure, a higher heart rate and sometimes tingling on the surface of the skin. Essentially, adrenaline physically puts the body on red alert for any emergency, by making changes that send more blood to muscles and more oxygen to lungs. The thrill of travelling at high speed is exactly the kind of experience that may trigger an adrenaline rush; revered car designer Frank Stephenson, the man behind the McLaren P1 and Ferrari 430, to name but a few, loves this feeling:

*In the right environment, such as a track, I love the adrenaline rush, it's such a natural high, it's a way of feeling alive ... more alive, in fact, because it is so physical.*

There are other more complex chemical reactions in the brain due to experiencing speed, such as the release of dopamine, such that regular doses can create a habit. It can be surmised that this could be a partial explanation as to why land speed record holders can't keep away from their machines, even when they are already the fastest in the world. There are many cases of people referring to themselves as speed addicts; this is often seen in racing drivers, such as Wendell Scott, the first African-American stock car driver, who was quoted in Brian Donovan's book, *Hard Driving*, saying how, 'Racing cars gets to be about like being a drug addict or an alcoholic. The more you do it, the more you like to do it.' In Diekstra and

Kroon's 1997 study, the authors suggest that 'drivers are experiencing a kind of narcotic effect, which can produce the same addictive response as more conventional drugs'. Hannah Elliott, revered journalist and commentator on speed and the automotive world, endorses this parallel:

*Speed is about perception and how your perception changes; that's also why people do drugs, because they want to change their perception of reality and their perception of the world. In that sense, I think it is easy to see how speed could be considered a type of drug.*

Former drag racer and fastest woman on a motorbike, Valerie Thompson openly admits that for her there is an addictive element:

*The fastest woman ever on a motorbike, land speed icon Valerie Thompson.*

*Oh gosh, it is so addictive. You want more. I got to 200 mph and immediately I said, 'Now I want to go 300 ...' I actually promised my husband I'd retire at 200, then I promised him at 300 and then 400, and now I keep saying I won't try for 500 mph but ...*

Another chemical element of the psychology of speed is testosterone. There is an argument in some medical quarters that due to higher levels of testosterone in males, men may be more aggressive and reckless around speed. In 2009, a study on organizational behaviour and human decision processes looked at the testosterone levels of men driving a sports car versus those using a sedan, in both empty streets and roads filled with women. The location and presence of women made virtually

no difference to the testosterone levels of either study group, but the men in the sports cars showed consistently higher levels than those in both sedan groups.

It's not just the release of hormones and chemicals that affect the individual at speed. With greater speed comes greater demands on the human body and senses. Land speed drivers have to cope with colossal forces on their bodies. At high velocity in a land speed car with the driver lying virtually prostrate, the blood rushes away from the legs and up into the torso and head, which can cause the driver to feel very dizzy - not ideal at speeds of 700 mph or more. Experts such as world land speed record holder Andy Green are able to tense certain muscle groups at exact moments, which helps to control the blood circulation in specific areas of the body, thus reducing the risk of fainting or dizziness. All the while they are doing this, they will also be handling all the technical demands of driving a land speed car travelling at extreme speed. If the blood pressure and physical demands become too much, then a process known as greying out first affects the eyes - then, worst case, it progresses to a blackout. Then, in the often sudden and extremely violent deceleration at the end

*Tachophobia is a fear of speed, an abnormal fear of going, or doing something, too fast. Extreme cases have been recorded where people are frightened by talking too fast, or eating too quickly. The fastest woman on a motorbike, Valerie Thompson, is not one of these people!*

of high-speed runs, the blood rushes back towards the legs, which can cause dizziness again. The dilemma is that if the driver tenses the wrong muscles too much or at the wrong time, there is a risk of actually increasing the chance of passing out. A further complication is what is known as somatogravic illusion, which is not related to driver seating. The inner ear provides us all with balance but, under extreme positive acceleration, the driver or pilot gets the impression that the vehicle's nose is rising. There have been instances of aircraft crashes due to somatogravic effects misleading the pilot. Land speed record cars tend to decelerate faster than they accelerate and Thrust2 was an extreme example – losing speed between 5 and 6 G. The somatogravic effect under extreme deceleration can cause the driver to believe that he or she is heading downhill into the centre of the earth. Richard Noble was totally unprepared for this, 'because you just wonder what the hell's going on and, of course, prior to these top speed runs I'd got no experience of this, so it's quite disconcerting but only for a second or two. The car was always safe as the brake parachute was giving us directional stability.'

Valerie Thompson explains how breathing is also crucial:

*There is actually something of a contradiction because, in many senses, the fastest riders are kind of the slowest humans. You've got to control your heart beat when you're on the starting line, you've got to breathe really well and in a controlled fashion. New riders are always coming up to me asking for advice, and the main thing I say to them all is: 'Get your breathing right.' That, and not doing a death clamp on the steering wheel!*

Obviously, only an elite few ultra-high-speed racers experience such physical extremes, but their reaction to, and handling of, such demands leads to the second domain of the psychology of speed: the developmental element. This is essentially how the brain and body are able to learn about speed and react to it in an increasingly refined manner. One classic example of this is how a racing driver develops the ability to slow down time. Racing drivers are habitually used to the manifold factors pressuring them when they are hurtling around a race track, certainly in ways that lesser drivers are not. For example, the 1992 Formula 1 world champion and 1993 Indy Car World Champion Nigel Mansell has first-hand, real world experience of what the scientists classify as velocity re-normalization. He told this author:

*When you are operating at the very highest level in any sport, your reflexes, senses and reaction times are acutely honed. This is the result of combining pure talent with thousands of hours of practice. It is said in some sports psychology circles that, aside from natural ability, luck and sheer determination, to perform a chosen sport to the skill level of a world champion you have to have practised that particular discipline for a minimum of 10,000 hours.*

For example, if a member of the public, rather than a professional tennis player, faced a serve from Roger Federer, the ball would fly past them virtually before they even realized he'd hit it. Yet his top-seeded rivals not only see that ball, but they are usually able to return it with venom. The same level of world-class skill applies to all sports at the highest levels, and Formula 1 is no exception. In my experience and opinion, an elite racing driver has the apparent ability to slow down time.

Mansell experienced this very early in his F1 career. Having worked his way through the ranks of various motorsport formulae, he had finally won a test seat with Colin Chapman's revered Lotus team, at the time a world leader. Accustomed to being the fastest man on track, Mansell was in for a very big shock when he rolled out onto the tarmac of the Paul Ricard circuit in France for his first test outing in a Lotus.

*You would think those first few laps in a Formula 1 car would've been the most exciting moment in my life, and that I would be stunned by the car's speed and performance. Not so. I was actually hugely disappointed and incredibly frustrated, even unnerved. It was a massive anticlimax. I didn't understand what was happening. Everything seemed to come at me so fast - the corners, the decisions, it was all just too quick. For example, I was going down the main straight okay but then having absolutely no time to go into the corners; it was all a blur. At the end of my session I was five or six seconds a lap off the pace. Five or six*

*Above and opposite: Formula 1 legend Nigel Mansell feared he would be unable to cope with the extreme speeds and physicality when he first jumped into a Lotus F1 car; by 1992, he was an idolised World Champion.*

*seconds - in Formula 1, five or six tenths of a second is a lifetime!*

*The grip never felt right and the gearbox was a real struggle, too. It was so disappointing. I thought the car would handle much better, have more grip, be nicer to drive and corner, but it was just ugly. At one point, the great Gilles Villeneuve came up behind me in his Ferrari so, of course, I let him past. Then I vainly tried to follow him. For a couple of the slower corners I was keeping up with him. That momentarily buoyed my spirits, but then he went around a fast corner lightning quick and, when I tried to follow him in the same manner, I span off. I remember just thinking, How the hell did he go around there that fast?*

Dejected, Mansell actually told his wife that night that he felt he wasn't cut out for

Formula 1; he simply could not see how he could acquire the skills to be that quick.

*The experience just didn't work for me. I thought,* This is a step too far – it doesn't work. *However, the next morning something amazing happened. The human brain is an incredible piece of technology. What had happened is that during the night, while I was consciously thinking about the events of the first day and later during my sleep too, my brain had upscaled and processed what it had witnessed the day before. Remarkably, within two laps on the following day, everything was different. The car was going faster in terms of absolute speed and grip levels were far higher due to grippier tyres, but to me it all seemed so much slower and easier to process. I was hitting 200 mph but I could see the trees going past, I could even pick out individual branches, as well as parts of the fencing and barriers. As the laps went by, it felt progressively slower and more manageable, even though my lap times were getting quicker.*

*My confidence soared; I started to feel the car instinctively, and within a few laps I was six seconds quicker than the day before. Then you think to yourself,* Well, that wasn't too hard after all! *It was such a huge relief.*

*Driving a Formula 1 car is all about having the time to make decisions. If you go into a corner and feel like you are doing 200 mph on the approach, then it is very hard to make the right decisions at the right time. Maybe a rival will try to overtake you or there could be oil on the track, bad weather, tyre wear, fuel worries and so on, there is a lot for your brain to compute, all at a viciously fast speed.*

*However, on that second day it all felt so much more ... 'leisurely' is not the right word, but certainly more manageable. I could see my racing line miles ahead; I could feel the track, change gear smoothly when I needed to, and so on. I suddenly knew I could do it. On that second day of testing, my brain had made all these adjustments.*

*Essentially, it means that F1 drivers are bending time. We are travelling at the same speed, the corners are coming up just as fast, but, in terms of our perception, time is moving slower than in reality. When you are really on top of your game, it is almost like racing flat out but in slow motion. You have more time to do the job. Your brain processes the information much quicker than the average person could do. Only then can you become at one with the car and the track.*

Dr Kerry Spackman is one of the world's leading neuroscientists and has worked with Formula 1 teams such as Jaguar and McLaren, assisting them with reconciling what their simulators are telling them versus what the drivers are feeling and reporting back. He has a clinical view on what Mansell is implying:

*If an ordinary person with no racing experience jumped in a Formula 1 car, their brain would be concentrating on moving their arms, legs, eyes, head, just to get the car around the track once. Each decision would need to be consciously made. Turn the wheel here; now the car is sliding so I need to correct that ... and so on. The problem is that the conscious part of the brain is very slow; it is a big overhead in terms of energy consumption, so therefore it is quite sluggish. The conscious circuits in the brain are not very precise; they are coarse and quite laborious, which, when you are driving a car at 200 mph, is not very helpful.*

*This is where practice comes in. Clinically, it has been proven that if you practise*

*something often enough, that process does an amazing thing - it switches from conscious to unconscious. There is a section at the back of the brain called the cerebellum, and when you practise the same activity or action thousands of times, this part of the brain recognizes that repetitive activity. Then, rather than consciously making a decision every time, it assumes that it would be far faster and more efficient to react subconsciously. When it makes that switch - from conscious to subconscious - the signals transmitted from your brain via your spinal cord to your arm to turn the steering wheel become an instantaneous, subconscious movement. You don't need to work out what to do every time. That is when you get really fast.*

*What this means is that the conscious part of the driver's brain is free and untaxed; it has lots of spare processing power because the subconscious part is doing the majority of the work. Therefore it can process the trees flying past; it can see faces in the crowd; it can see the pit lane as if it is going past at only 40 mph. The brain has room to spare. It can make decisions in a race in a millisecond, yet almost leisurely. This is why champion drivers can indeed seem to slow down time.*

Sports mind coach Don MacPherson explains how motorsport teams try to circumvent this slow process of endless repetition:

*Simulators can accelerate the process of the brain being tuned to accommodate speed more readily and efficiently. However, the brain needs* to be tuned during real-world runs, as well as by working with mind coaches away from the simulator, who are able to hone and refine the thought processes.

Land speed legend Richard Noble, who broke the overall record in 1983 with his average of 633.468 mph across the measured mile, explains some of the very peculiar sensory challenges that occur when travelling at such high speed:

*When you are driving very, very fast, your mind is processing the data so rapidly that in point of fact it appears that you can see every single detail on the track come up and go underneath the car. I mean every detail, every rock, every line in the surface, it's incredible. Your mental processes speed right up so that everything happens in slow motion. Of course, your thinking has always to be ahead of the car ...*

What is fascinating about the land speed driver's processing of speed compared to that of a racing driver is that the general consensus is that the brain can only slow down time in this way after thousands of repetitions, day after day, week after week, year after year of going around tracks all over the world. But land speed cars usually only run a few times – in the case of Sir Henry Segrave and the 1927 Golden Arrow, essentially only once. So the window for the driver to learn and process speed in that actual car is miniscule. Noble ran Thrust2 around sixty times. In 2019, F1 teams in pre-season testing would manage 24,000 miles, in eight days, averaging 300 miles per day per car (at least

seventy laps and often as many as 130). Therefore, a crucial and slightly troubling part of this phenomenon is that this superhuman-like ability to slow down time could be borne out of this endless repetition. Yet for most people buying an extremely fast road car, there has been no such repeated practice: a daily commute to work and maybe a sprinkling of track days each year might be the average, while even an amateur club racer cannot profess to have as much experience as a professional. Yet, in theory, anyone is able to purchase modern vehicles capable of racing car speeds without specialist training or prescribed skill requirements other than a standard driving licence. In that sense, it is clear that while we admire racing drivers for their bravery and courage on track, driving to the race circuit to watch them may be far more dangerous.

Clearly land speed drivers have a different accommodation for speed but, at the same time, there are individuals in everyday life who love speed while others hate it. Speed means different things to different people. Why is this?

The subjectivity of people's personal experiences of speed is immense. A massive element of this divide is also perhaps the single most prominent aspect of speed: fear. To someone who has never driven in a car or similar vehicle, 50 mph would feel lightning quick. Former land speed record holder Richard Noble, when asked if he ever thought he might die, dismisses the notion:

*Me? No, I didn't feel like that at all. You take the decision right at the start of the project, 'Okay, we are going to do this, let's put all that worry behind us and just get on with the job.' Later, however, the severity of any potential crash does hit home. You always believe you are going to be the record holder. But there is this extraordinary feeling when you come to the end of the run - and I discussed this with Andy Green once - when you fling open the cockpit hatch, get some fresh air in and think, Hey, I'm still alive, fantastic!*

However, in line with the neuroscientific explanations above, there are individuals who are so used to high speed that their brain has quite literally become accustomed to the sensation, which means that to a degree their experience of speed is actually more muted. Acclaimed designer Frank Stephenson had a remarkable experience when he was chief designer at Ferrari:

*I was in a car with Dario Benuzzi, the head test driver for Ferrari. He has this reputation of being very cool but behind that it is a fact that he was as quick on the Ferrari test track in Fiorano as a lot of the professional drivers that race for a living. He picked me up from Bologna airport the day before I had my interviews with Montezemolo for the design job at Ferrari. He was in a prototype 599 with wires sticking out of everywhere inside the cabin. There is a stretch of highway before you turn off for Modena and I think he just wanted to scare me a little bit. He was in complete control of the car even though it was January, in cold rain so it could have been*

*icy, he was wearing sunglasses - at night - and smoking. Cool as ice and totally calm. What was interesting to me was that I wasn't scared either, I knew he was in control. So maybe the fear of speed is a fear of losing control?*

There is a strange dichotomy in speed - the adrenaline comes from feeling almost out of control, yet the records are set by people who remain in control, because otherwise the results could be catastrophic. Hannah Elliott expands on this idea and suggests that this fear of losing control might be why speed appeals to some:

*In my opinion, it has to do with the possibility of death - that is a very human fascination or urge. When you are presented with the possibility of death, it actually affirms life. Therefore, when we have these brilliant, courageous drivers who are flirting with death, achieving speeds that most of us can't even imagine, it's like they're touching something that we all want to know. We are all kind of curious about that dynamic. By contrast, speed frightens some people because they feel like they're not in control but that is also tied to their fear of death.*

For some of the land speed racers, it is not just the top speed title that appeals; many have admitted that it is the attraction of the unknown, of not knowing for certain what will happen when travelling on land quicker than any human being has ever done before. Many people see this as an intensely fearful experience; land speed record holders see it very simply as an exciting challenge.

Eminent mind coach Don McPherson has worked with many motorsport champions and extreme speed athletes, and believes that fear in this context is often misunderstood:

*It is a fear of losing control, not a fear of speed. That's what separates people in this sphere. The control of fear, the internal instinct to protect oneself, is absolutely crucial to any record attempt. What we are talking about here is the need to control that inner dialogue, that voice that is telling you to slow down, be more safe. Essentially, these speed record holders are able to reprogram their internal software, override that instinct. If that interferes with their attempt to go faster than any human before, then the record will not be broken, no matter how fast the machine is. It's about mind management; they are able to tune their brains to compute these ridiculously fast speeds in a way that is calm, measured and controlled - as much as it can be. Personality traits can really interfere at this crucial moment: that can come from a number of sources. Poverty as a child, anxiety from a traumatic experience, maybe they witnessed a bad accident where someone they love was hurt, there can be almost infinite reasons but these all impact on the personality, and when humans are competing at these extreme envelopes of known high speed performance, the minutest of margins make the difference.*

According to *The Atlantic* magazine, this divergence in perception of an individual's experience of speed can be down to both the clinical neuroscience and also any potential for rewarding moments - the article suggests that people's reactions to fear can vary hugely due to their brain chemistry such as the previously discussed dopamine levels, and this means that certain people get more of a kick out of high speed than others. Further, it suggests that unlike, say, a haunted house attraction at a funfair, where the customer ultimately knows they are safe, in a speed situation it is entirely possible that serious injury or worse may occur. Yet some individuals still seek out and even actively pursue this buzz.

According to Richard Noble:

*Fear is very interesting. Fear can be a dangerous, controlling element. The key point about fear is this: if you are going to do something like drive a land speed record car, then you've got to simply put the fear behind you; if you get frightened, then you've got to stop because you are a risk to everybody. You could be an absolutely enormous liability. There are two extremes that can happen to a person who gets frightened: one is that he or she becomes timid, in which case you are not going to deliver for your team; the other is that they get a fix, overcoming personal fear can create a terrific buzz but that means that, fired up with the obsession, they've got to go back and overcome it again and again - in which case, as a driver, you are even more dangerous because you are not driving as a member of the team, you are doing it for yourself and sooner or later you are going to push too far ...*

Land speed racer and drag motorbike record holder Valerie Thompson concurs:

'When you are trying to beat your own land speed record, almost everybody asks the question, "Why the hell you are doing it if you hold the record already?" to which I would always answer, "Ah, but we've got the Americans on our backs, we have to win, we love a fight!"'

Richard Noble OBE

*I'm in the business of taking risks, my passion is speed, I'm all about the speed but I'm also all about being in control, building the strength and the confidence in me, my vehicle, and my team. That can affect your control over fear. The most important aspect to going fast is managing your fears. Understanding the limits of your machine is critical, managing the risk is a key to success but managing your fear is instrumental. Fear will upset the whole entire run, fear will damage your thinking, it will slow down your reactions, it will damage the control of where you are going, where your heart's at. It can do a lot of damage.*

Richard Noble suggests that, although any land speed car is obsessively detailed and engineered, there is still the human factor, which will always remain a big a part of the puzzle:

*The question is which are the limitations that are going to be hit first? Are they the driver's limitations or the car's limitations? If it's the*

*driver limitations, then you've simply got to stop and say, 'I'm frightened, I'm not up for this,' and the team have to regroup. For my part, people ask me if I used to get frightened and the honest answer is no, not really. I was just too damn busy.*

There are also very direct sensory elements of high speed that affect an individual's perception - and potential fear - of the speed experience. For example, Noble details the intense sensory experience of these mighty machines:

*You build these cars as part of the dream experience but of course that vehicle is dead until you start the engine. It takes a long time to build so you understand all the systems and every square inch of it but when you start the engine (or engines!), everything instantly changes because of the incredible noise and the enormous power that's unleashed. It has been said that BloodhoundSSC when fitted with its jet and rocket motors will be fifteen times louder than a 747 at take off!*

For many people, such an apocalyptic level of noise would be deeply frightening; for Noble, it was all part of the buzz, and a signal that it was time for him to go to work.

*Thrust2's chassis was based around the space-frame concept, coincidentally first seen in road cars with the 1954 Mercedes 300SL Gullwing.*

Expanding on the idea of being out of control as either a negative or positive depending on the individual, designer Frank Stephenson continues:

*I very much love speed, because it heightens your senses. Going slow also does that, so basically anything in between going fast and going slow is a waste of time. There is an element of danger to speed but I like speed with a certain amount of control, I'm not in it just to scare the hell out of myself. I don't like going fast on public roads and in that environment you might be in control but other people aren't necessarily so. Your experience of speed also depends on the environment: if you are doing 300 kph on a high-speed track, then it doesn't necessarily feel that fast because you have very few reference points; if you do the same speed on a motorway, with cars and lorries passing you, barriers buildings and so on, then it feels incredibly fast. Yet it is the same speed.*

For some people, speed is only rewarding when experienced proactively, for example when they are driving. For others, such as Stephenson, speed is consistently exhilarating even in different forms:

*For me, speed is enjoyable in different ways whether passive or active. I fly a lot and I'm one of those people that likes to look out of the window as we are accelerating for take-off,*

*to see and feel the acceleration, like I'm still a 10-year-old. I must have taken hundreds and hundreds of flights over the years and yet I still get a thrill from that moment.*

Asked if his record-breaking top speed runs have ever scared him in any way, Le Mans winner Andy Wallace had this to say:

*It's weird because I've raced for well over 30 years professionally and when you go into a race, you have an apprehension - you can call it nerves if you want, but you are certainly well aware that what you are about to do is dangerous and potentially something bad could happen. However, you know the science and that the clever people have been eliminating the risk to an absolute minimum amount but the risk still is there, so ... I don't know if you can call it afraid, but perhaps there is an element of that.*

*For international race-winner Andy Wallace, driving a road vehicle that has greater straight line speed than his Le Mans winning race cars is a striking mental challenge.*

There is a school of thought that early formative experiences indelibly affect a person's experience of speed. The renowned Swiss psychologist Jean Piaget was famed for his pioneering theory of cognitive development, which studied and tried to explain the evolution and nature of human intelligence. He believed that speed overcame endurance in the human psyche, and that a person's relationship with speed begins with formative experiences as a child. To extrapolate this notion, if a young child experiences a positive, exciting event involving speed, perhaps with praise or encouragement from parents or peers, then there is a logic that their developing brain associates that as an experience to be repeated; by contrast, if a child is

perhaps involved in a frightening accident due to speed, with subsequent distress, admonishment or even injury, then there is a possibility that the opposite is true. Writer Hannah Elliott has a personal take on this theory:

*My first memory - period - is one of speed. I remember running on a track when I was about three and I vividly recall the feeling of moving through space at a speed faster than I normally operated at, it was just sheer joy. I remember the warm sun and just this feeling of moving through space at speed. Okay, it wasn't behind a wheel but that was my first memory, and when I recall that, the overriding feeling is one of speed. That feels embedded in my very cells, somehow.*

This brings the discussion to another domain of psychology of speed: the social and personality trait of speed. This book has already touched on the social impact of speed with groups such as the Ton Up Boys, and how teenagers have found fast cars an almost irresistible temptation for decades. Wrapped up alongside the thrill of fast driving for some individuals is the impact that may have on their social acceptance or stature. Cars are inextricably linked through popular culture and social perceptions to success, power and even virility. Racer John Morrison readily admits that many of the racers he competed against in the 1970s and 1980s started off driving fast in order to increase their chances with girls; that may not be politically correct, but it is his personal experience. The social elevation of an alpha male crossing a finish line first in a street drag race is one obvious benefit of this dynamic. This in turn may affect many individual's self-perception - a race lost, a worse car, less horsepower etc - may rightly or wrongly diminish a person's stature in a social group, as well as their own self-esteem to a degree. This isn't to suggest that any such consequences are appropriate, but they are commonplace.

The above factors in the psychology of speed are the subject of much debate and certainly there is no cast-iron, definitive answer to many of the questions these arguments provoke. Speed can have an enormous impact - positive and negative - on an individual's psychology and therefore life experience. The reasons for that are complex, multi-layered and not always consistent. What is clear is that every individual's experience of speed, and the psychology around that phenomenon, is unique.

Valerie Thompson's Target 550 streamliner car.

# Chapter 17

# Top Speed with Top Fuel

*If everything seems under control, you're not going fast enough.*

Mario Andretti

When looking for the modern world's most savage expression of speed, is there a more pure and brutal manifestation than drag racing? It is fair to say that land speed cars travel to a much higher top speed, but given the context of drag racing - on a relatively thin strip of track with barriers to the side, battling not just the clock but also a fellow competitor just a few metres away, watched on by vast crowds and with hot dog stands doing good business nearby – what drag cars do in terms of pure speed is absolutely astounding and, to a degree, every bit as shocking as the extremes of land speed records.

Drag racing has its roots in the same flat-out, foot-to-the-floor extreme personalities of land speed merchants. Initially small pockets of largely outlaw, underground racers (not as yet called hot rodders) in the 1930s tested their engines and mettle by engaging in straight line speed races with their tuned

*Starter Frank Bowman leaps into the air to begin a drag race at an old US Air Force base in Florida, 1954.*

daily driver, often on two-lane public roads; obviously this soon attracted the attention of law enforcement officers. Worse still, some of the more deviant elements created on-road games of danger that were verging on suicidal, as *Driving Line* magazine recounted:

*Games included 'Chicken', where two opposing cars would accelerate toward each other to see who would spook first; 'Crinkle-fender', where moving cars would hit each other without wrecking; and 'Pedestrian Poker', where a driver tried to brush (but not actually hit) pedestrians. The public was getting fed up.*

The racers therefore graduated to the dry lake beds of 1930s California, such as in the Mojave Desert on the Muroc lake. Early pioneers such as California-based gas station owner and mechanic C. J. Pappy Hart and Creighton Hunter recognized that road racing was too dangerous and joined forces with others to attempt to legitimize what was essentially illegal street racing. Another speed freak, Wally Parks, a military tank test-driver for General Motors who served in the army in the South Pacific in the Second World War, set up the Road Runners Club in 1937 and would eventually become a leading light in the sport (he helped organize the very first Speed Week at the Bonneville Salt Flats in 1949). The emphasis soon began to move away from top speeds and towards quicker acceleration.

It wasn't until after the war that the sport began to blossom, often populated by

*Top fuel dragsters are the world's quickest accelerating race cars, hitting more than 300 mph in just over three seconds. Racers such as three-time world champion Antron Brown experience launch forces in excess of 8 G.*

young racers who had served as mechanics in the conflict and emerged with vast engineering knowledge. Quickly, more and more racers were drawn to the increasingly regulated and organized meets. Just as many of their European counterparts utilized the now-disused runways and airfields of the post-war world, US drag racers found these long, flat strips of land ideal for their blatant and unashamed pursuit of pure speed. Also, like the Bentley Boys before them, these pioneering drag racers would often drive to their track to compete in simple, often home-modified cars.

The exact origins of the term 'drag racing' are unclear. Common theories include the fact that racers competed on paved sections in smaller towns known as the main drag; racers often dared rivals to 'drag their car out of the shop' so they could race; and sometimes, to maximize revs, drivers would hold a car in gear longer, known as 'dragging'.

By 1951, there was a sufficiently burgeoning scene that the National Hot Rod Association was formed (with Wally Parks as the first president), holding its first official race in April 1953 on a slice of the Los Angeles County Fairgrounds parking lot in Pomona. It wasn't long before the first star cars and celebrity racers began to emerge, with substantial crowds flocking to every event. So complex and varied were the numerous cars that the sport necessarily began to splinter into a number of categories, according to axle ratios, year, make, engine

displacements and safety equipment – at the time of writing, there are groups such as Top Fuel, Pro Stock, Top Alcohol Dragster, Pro Stock Motorbike and the highly misleading Funny Cars. There is little humour, though, about the latter land bullets, which may resemble road cars in some distorted, cartoon form but can hit 330 mph in less than 4 seconds. Car manufacturers such as Ford and Chrysler came on board, and the engineering evolved to such extremes that the world's very best speed minds were recruited by, and championed within, the world of drag racing. Turbo-fuels such as nitromethane ('nitro' is a compound that requires very little oxygen to burn at a very high rate) led to speeds becoming increasingly unprecedented and shockingly quick, so they polarized opinion; these controversial fuels would be banned and then readmitted. In 1963, the first serious televised races projected the sport to a nationwide level, as drag racing entered its modern era. The attraction of extreme speed was both a spectator draw and one that generated TV advertising, so at this point drag racing was very much a modern commercial commodity. With that came investment, and with the influx of money came ... even greater speeds.

Extreme speed is about the only way to describe what these phenomenal drag racing machines can do. Top Fuel dragsters are the quickest-accelerating racing cars in the world. These machines move so quickly from a standing start that it is almost pointless to measure a 0-60 mph time; 0-100 mph is 0.8 seconds; they can surpass 280 mph in 200 metres; and they are capable of hitting 335 mph in less than 4 seconds (generating an average of 4 Gs in the process). Their name is derived from the mix of fuel they use, which consists of 90 per cent nitro methane and 10 per cent alcohol, generating far more power than conventional petrol-fuelled vehicles. In fact, they travel so fast that these astonishing machines have long needed parachutes to slow them down after their brief run is complete.

Of course, with these incomprehensible speeds comes severe danger. The first decades of drag racing saw front-engined cars dominate; however, in 1971, a car driven by Don Garlit suffered a massive transmission failure and explosion which split the car in half and cut his right foot off. Garlit recuperated, then developed and built Swamp Rat XIV, the first successful rear-engined dragster - the standard car layout from thereon. Fifteen years later, Garlit topped 270 mph in his streamlined Swamp Rat XXX which, twelve months later, was enshrined in the National Museum of American History - essentially meaning that this former outlaw drag racing phenomenon was now fully accepted by the US establishment. In 1992, former Funny Car racer Kenny Bernstein took his Top Fuel drag car to the first 300 mph pass in NHRA history. On board these Top Fuel monsters is usually an engine with around 8000 hp, although some go as high as 10,000 hp, with 6000 foot-pounds of torque!

It's not just cars that obliterate the quarter-mile on a drag strip. Motorbikes are also a key part of this extreme speed world. Valerie Thompson, the world's fastest woman on a motorbike, also enjoys a career in drag racing. Valerie's explanation of the extreme and ultra-intense experience on the drag strip is hugely insightful for fans of speed:

*Every time I'm on the starting line at a racing event, I feel the passion, the excitement, I feel the monster of adrenaline. It's like you are a monster on that race track. In drag racing, you race against the competition in the next lane, they are right there alongside you, in that sense it is the closest form of racing on the planet. That brings an extra level of intensity and adrenaline to the experience. There is a lot talked about in terms of the super-rapid acceleration and top speeds, but actually so much is about the speed of reaction time of the driver. These are races that can be won by a few thousandths of a second. So you can have the fastest car or bike at the race, but if your reactions are too slow, then you will not win.*

*When I went 7.06 seconds in a quarter of a mile, I literally thought I messed up, I didn't shift on time, something happened to the bike that upset the balance, yet that piece of paper validates what I did, that's history. That was the most thrilling ride I ever had. Funnily enough, I thought it was the slowest run I had done, but it ended up the fastest!*

*The Shockwave Jet Truck holds the world record for jet-powered full-sized trucks at 376 mph, completing the quarter-mile in 6.63 seconds.*

With drag racing, it's all over in five or six seconds, that is perhaps the most intense manifestation of speed because of the brevity of what happens. The motorcycles are going six/seven seconds in a quarter of a mile, for two wheels ... that's fast. The g-force is about 3.5 Gs on the starting line. Consequently, your upper body strength in the core is so important. In addition, your leg strength is vital because you've got to hold the bike standing exactly upright, you've got to keep it solid, you can't move around, because if you lean to the right even slightly, then you're going to go to the right when you launch that motorcycle, and that is not going to end well. I've learned that lesson the hard way ... People often ask me to explain the acceleration. It's hard to precisely do that, because it is so extreme, but what I will say is that it is like your heart being slammed into your feet. There is so much horsepower, so much grip, the forces at play are astonishing and to feel that moment of launch is just incredible. These things are LOUD, too. When you sit on a drag bike, you hear everything, but then the strangest thing happens when you get up to that light ... I hear no fans, I hear no other bikes, no people around me, it is suddenly silent and pure. It feels like it's in slow motion. It's actually an incredibly calming experience.

It seems this extreme experience is also one that the public cannot get enough of – the fact that the NHRA has 70,000 members, 120 tracks and 40,000 licensed competitors indicates not only how popular drag racing is, but also American society's continuing obsession with speed. Although drag racing enjoys pockets of international appeal, such as in Australasia, South America and South Asia, it remains a predominantly American-led sport, but that aside, the speeds that these machines can achieve mark them out as truly astonishing players in the history of speed.

Drag bikes can boast up to 1,500hp and are capable of hitting 200 mph in less than 660 feet.

# Chapter 18

# The Gender of
# Speed

*Teach her that the idea of 'gender roles' is absolute nonsense. Do not ever tell her that she should or should not do something because she is a girl. 'Because you are a girl' is never a reason for anything. Ever.*

Author Chimamanda Ngozi Adichie

The world of drag racing has actually been one of the highest profile speed arenas for women to compete equally alongside men. Valerie Thompson is not the only female to succeed on the drag strip - other women include Carol Burkett, Shirley Muldowney and Leah Pritchett. However, a quick glance at the record books will tell you that there has never been an outright land speed record held by a woman; similarly, there has never been a female Formula 1 World Champion or, for that matter, female champions in world rallying, British touring cars, NASCAR ... there seems to be a pattern here. The statistics are just as stark in the wider world of automotive manufacture; until Mary Barra took the post of CEO of General Motors in 2013, there had never been a female boss of a major car manufacturer. And in 2016, only 11 per cent of the global workforce in the automotive industry were women.

The clear gender bias in the history of speed has arguably worsened, not improved, since the early days of the story. In the formative years of motor cars, women played a crucial role; after all, as previously detailed, the very first car journey was made by Karl Benz's wife, Bertha, who was frustrated by her husband's tentative testing approach. Yet her husband did not invent the car just for men. His ambition was to create a vehicle capable of transforming personal mobility, regardless of gender. The car is, after all, a genderless and inanimate object, therefore any gender limitations that have been associated with the car - and speed - have been imposed by society.

Although the first speed pioneers were not exclusively men, there was a distinct weighting in favour of male participants. The first recorded race with female competitors wasn't until the late 1890s, when a group of Parisian women charged around a horse track on their motorized tricycles. Women did have access to automobiles, but even so there were early signs that the world of speed was already being perceived as a male domain. A contemporary *Country Life* article described

*Camille du Gast in Berlin, 1901.*

electric cars as perfectly suited to the needs of women, who travelled shorter distances, stayed nearer to home and needed an 'ever ready run-about for daily use, leaving extended travel and fast driving to the men in gas powered cars'. Practicalities were sometimes put forward as to why women were better kept as passengers - for example, before the advent of the starter motor, cranking a car was often cited as a physical barrier to women using vehicles; in fact, cranking some cars correctly did not necessarily need huge strength, but more a timing and understanding of exactly where to hold the crank.

Yet a more objective foray into the historical archives reveals a long and colourful cast of women obsessed with speed and hugely talented at achieving it. Take Camille du Gast, a wealthy Frenchwoman who was an accomplished parachute jumper, fencer, skier, rifle and pistol shot, horse trainer, concert pianist and singer as well as extreme sports enthusiast - she made her name in 1901 by starting the Paris–Berlin race last out of 122 cars, yet drove her massive Panhard-Levassor so brilliantly she finished thirty-

*Dorothy Levitt driving an enormous 26 hp Napier at Brooklands in 1908.*

third, later expressing disappointment in her ability to 'only' overtake eighty-nine competitors. She was the first woman to consistently race at a top international level and attracted much media attention, earning her the tag of 'the Amazon with green eyes' and 'the Valkyrie of the motor car'. She was also renowned for leaping to the aid of fellow racers who had crashed, on more than one occasion saving the lives of competitors by hauling them out of their wreckage. When French law banned women from competing in auto-racing in 1904, the wording used in her specific case highlighted 'inexperience' and 'feminine excitability' (by 1914, there were still only 100 driving licences issued to Frenchwomen). So Camille turned to high speed boating instead. After an attempt

on her life, rumoured to be masterminded by her daughter's ruthless friends who were sniffing a large inheritance, du Gast retired and devoted the rest of her life to campaigning for women's rights, helping disadvantaged children and destitute women, and promoting animal welfare.

Dorothy Levitt is considered to be the very first English female racing driver. She actually competed initially on water then started racing cars in 1903 while still working as a secretary, almost immediately winning her class at the Southport Speed Trial in a Gladiator. The following year saw her become the first ever female works

174

driver, in a Napier. Her most famous victory was when she won her class at the Autocar Challenge Trophy in an 80 hp Napier in 1905. She then became the first ever female land speed record holder when she hit 90.88 mph in a 100 hp Napier, which saw the media describe her as the fastest girl on earth - she later set this record higher, at 96 mph. Levitt would later make another mark by inventing the rear-view mirror, although her early prototypes were simply hand-held pieces of mirrored glass in the cockpit!

Opportunities for women in the first decade or so of the new century remained scarce, but after the First World War more openings began to emerge, with famous names such as Maria Antonietta d'Avanzo and Eliška Junková making headlines with their blistering speed performances. The best place achieved by a woman at Le Mans is fourth, secured by Odette Siko in 1932, racing an Alfa Romeo 6C in the 2-litre class. Two years earlier she had competed with Marguerite Mareuse as the first ever all-female crew. One of their contemporaries, Margaret Allan, became one of only a handful of women to drive at over 120 mph around Brooklands two years later. Women had not been allowed to race at that famous circuit until 1908, a restriction justified by the fact that there were no female jockeys either. When this regulation was eventually repealed, it was done so with the condition that female racers tie cords around their bodies to hold their skirts in place, because 'it would have been very improper to show one's knees aboard a car

that was already stripped of any bodywork and which could not have hidden anything'. It would be well into the 1920s before Brooklands would allow mixed racing, and even then only with a male mechanic attached.

Immediately after the First World War, female drivers boomed somewhat - while many of their husbands had been away fighting, these women had taken up driving ambulances, taxis, lorries and sometimes military vehicles, in the process creating a new generation of very capable drivers. By the twenties, women had entered the work force in unprecedented numbers and had gained the right to vote, yet the pervading discrimination continued. In his essay, 'The Automobile and Gender', M. Wachs wrote:

*Conservative social movements - those who wanted to preserve and protect traditional gender roles - naturally found themselves rather aggressively countering the threat of the automobile by reasserting the centrality of traditional roles and integrating the automobile into the nurturing and child-rearing activities that were traditionally associated with women. Members of the clergy often wrote about and prepared sermons about the dangerous social consequences of the automobile, which included opportunities for young women to escape supervision in ways that would certainly lead to moral decline.*

The contradictions continued: in 1922, Henry Ford opened Phoenix Mill and began recruiting widows and single women, giving them equal pay to the men - but only 'so they could dress attractively and get married'. Later, American expressionist painter and author Hilda Ward recounted that she found it annoying that her chauffeur (who she suggested was a social inferior) assumed to know more about cars than she did.

Canadian Kay Petre, using a 2-litre supercharged Bugatti, stunned sceptical men at Brooklands during the 1930s, including setting the Mountain Class Circuit F fastest lap as well as a record at Shelsley Walsh. She would often arrive at Brooklands by aeroplane with her aviator husband, wearing her trademark light blue overalls, jump into a race car and thunder around the track before returning home airborne - earning her the name of the Brooklands 'Speed Queen'. The diminutive 4'10" former ice-skating champion Petre once drove a huge 10.5-litre V-12 Delage while sitting on a custom-made bolster cushion, aided by wooden blocks attached to the accelerator, brake and clutch so she could reach them. Her career was eventually ended after a serious multi-car crash left her with severe injuries and in a coma. 'When you practise a dangerous sport like racing,' reflected Petre, 'you always risk paying the price one day.'

Brooklands seems to have been a hub of speed-obsessed women. The fastest woman ever around that famous track was Gwenda Stewart, who hit 136 mph in 1935, four years before the circuit closed. These women were still in a significant minority, even though a consumer study at the time stated that 41 per cent of all car purchases had women as the principal buyer.

This highlights a contradiction between the evolution of speed and the commerce of the motor car. In the Roaring Twenties, women were very much in the minds of motor manufacturers, at least in terms of the purchasing decision. As well as music hall stars, musicians and film stars, high-profile women were often invited to celebrated races to attract the all-important publicity for various marques. This did not, however, suggest that the male-dominated world of speed was moving towards a more equitable role for women: 'Owing to their inferior motor outlets,' wrote one contemporary journalist in 1932, 'women succeed best in relatively simple motor activities, such as sweeping, washing, and ironing, rather than more complex motor tasks like driving.'

Yet remarkable female racers and speed merchants continued to make their mark. Earlier, this book touched on the remarkable cabaret dancer turned racer Hellé Nice, known as the Bugatti Queen, who became the first female winner of a Grand Prix; her contemporary, Violette Morris, has a story that is even stranger than fiction. This daughter of a French army general was an openly gay Olympic discus thrower, water polo champion and boxer who regularly fought and beat men in the ring. She was also an accomplished athlete, then graduated to cycling races and eventually motorbikes and cars. All this despite voraciously smoking

Canadian racer and writer Kay Petre often flew into
Brooklands and was known as the 'Speed Queen'.

three packets of American cigarettes every day. After driving ambulances on the slopes of the Somme during the First World War, she became entranced by speed and took up motor racing. Morris won gold in the discus and shot put at the 1924 Olympics, but was stopped from competing at the 1928 Olympics due to the onerous and draconian social reaction to her sexuality, with authorities citing her masculine dress sense and open homosexuality as sufficient reason to prevent her representing her country. Instead she threw herself into motor racing and very quickly proved to be extremely talented. Most shockingly, Morris underwent an elective double mastectomy so that she could better fit into the cramped cockpits of the early racing cars of the period. Her later life is tainted by stories of Nazi involvement as a spy (according to the brilliant book, *Fast Ladies*, by Jean-François Bouzanquet, one of her nicknames was 'the

Hyena of the Gestapo'). Her controversial and striking life ended when her car was ambushed by armed members of the French Resistance in a quiet country road.

When the Second World War took men to The Front, the car manufacturing plants back at home were largely kept operational by the women they had left behind. The turn signal, stop light and windscreen wiper were all designed by women, yet the first female automotive head designer didn't follow until 1943. In the 1950s, General Motors' Harley J. Earl set up an all-female design team, reinforcing the notion that good design is good design, regardless of gender. Yet after the Second World War, government advertising campaigns often exhorted women to stay at home and raise children, look after returning spouses who had been at The Front and keep clear of the distractions of driving. One contemporary review of the Mercedes 300SL Gullwing, from *Car and Driver* in 1956, said, 'I cannot see it as anything but a man's machine. It's too hairy a beast for a woman to drive unless she's a fairly brawny athlete.' Further, a generation of pre-war female racers were now a decade older and so there was something of a dearth

*General Motors' pioneering design team in the 1950s; by contrast, in 1955, Dodge launched the La Femme, a pink, two-door coupé for women, featuring a matching calf-skin purse with coordinated accessories such as a face-powder compact, lipstick case, cigarette case, comb, cigarette lighter and change purse.*

of new names to excite the public, as well as a less than encouraging environment for speed-obsessed women.

From the 1950s onwards, a long line of female trailblazers have proved time and again that women – given an equal opportunity – were perfectly capable of driving very fast. Sara Christian competed in the first NASCAR race in 1949 and remains the only woman to secure a top five finish in that sport. The world of Formula 1 saw its first woman compete in 1958 at the Belgian Grand Prix, when Maria Teresa de Filippis finished tenth. But she was not allowed to race at the following French Grand Prix, when the race director was alleged to have told her that, 'the only helmet a woman should wear is the one at the hairdressers'.

Denise McCluggage, a journalist who became the first woman to win the Monte Carlo Rally, sported a white helmet with red polka dots and became famous for driving Porsches very fast. Having studied philosophy and political economics, she became a photo journalist and covered American motoring races, leading to her obsession with going fast (her success in rallying is mirrored by that of racers such as Pat Moss-Carlsson, Michelle Moulton and Anne Hall).

The first lady of drag racing, Shirley Muldowney, is the daughter of a former prize fighter. After telling her father that she was being bullied at school due to her diminutive frame, he advised her to: 'Pick up a board, you pick up a pipe, you pick up a brick, and you part their hair with it.' She first found out her penchant for speed as a street racer in her teens in New York and even crept out of the house in her pyjamas to attend late night races. She quickly entered drag racing, albeit at a time when female racers were largely unheard of, yet her bravery and breath-taking speed in the highly dangerous Funny Car series saw her survive a number of horrific fiery accidents, including a 1973 wreck that required serious burns rehabilitation. Despite this, she won eighteen national events in the 1960s. Fiercely competitive, Shirley simply left Funny Cars and moved up to Top Fuel, the ultimate drag racing machines. Here she took the Top Fuel Championship three times. So well-known was Shirley in the 1970s that many fans of the sport regarded her as famous as stunt rider Evel Knievel.

Another horrendous accident in 1984 nearly cost Shirley her life, but she returned after a lengthy and painful rehabilitation to set more records, ensuring she was later inducted into the American Motorsport Hall of Fame, the International Motor Sports Hall of Fame and to the NHRA Top 50 Drivers of 1951–2000.

Italian racer Lella Lombardi initially learnt her skills behind the wheel of the local butcher's van, because neither of her parents could drive. She was a prodigious multi-sports competitor who came to racing late, in her twenties, but quickly proved to have tremendous skill and strength in handling very physical and extremely

The First Lady of Drag Racing,
Shirley Muldowney, in 1973.

dangerous racing cars. Known for her no-nonsense approach, she did not claim back costly travel expenses from her team (very unusually for racing drivers) and never travelled with an entourage. In 1974, she became the first woman to score F1 points, with a sixth place at the Spanish Grand Prix, but she scored only half a point rather than the customary full point, as the race was stopped short of half distance. 'I don't think it dawned on me that I was the very first woman to collect championship points. Things like that just don't worry me. I'm just as competitive as any male, in my mind.'

Former flight instructor and aerospace engineer Janet Guthrie got her flying licence aged just seventeen. Beginning work in research and development for an aviation company, specifically on programmes that became precursors to Project Apollo, Guthrie then qualified as a potential candidate for NASA's astronaut programme.

Her entry into the world of racing started when she bought a Jaguar XK120 coupé, and began competing in hill climbs and field trials. Her tenacious and rapid racing style quickly saw her climb up the racing ladder

*Elation on the face of Janet Guthrie after an inspired run at the Indy 500 in 1978.*

*Another trail-blazing woman in the history of speed, the remarkable Bunny Burkett.*

such that, by 1976, she became the first woman to race a NASCAR superspeedway event. Talking to the *Washington Post* in 2006, Guthrie said, 'I knew the woman part was irrelevant, but nobody else seemed to. I am a racer right through to my bone marrow, and that's what it was all about for me.'

As mentioned, drag racing has boasted many successful female competitors - Carol 'Bunny' Burkett was nicknamed so because of her previous work at the Playboy Club of Baltimore as a hostess, which she needed to do to finance her racing. She adopted the tag and even had the artwork on her cars, and remains the only woman to have won an IHRA Alcohol

Funny Car drag race championship, in 1984. In 1995, her rival's drag car crashed across the track, hitting Burkett's then catapulting her into woods at 200 mph, resulting in injuries so severe that her doctors decreed she would never walk again. Within 18 months, she was back in a drag car, racing once more. After a remarkable career breaking records and winning races, Bunny sadly passed away in April 2020, aged 75. Her family said at the time: 'We are sad that she made it to the finish line first, but we ALL know she'd have had it no other way.'

Other notable stars included the Queen of the Ring, Sabine Schmitz, who is said to have lapped the Nürburgring over 25,000 times; Danica Patrick repeatedly breaking records in Indy, including a third place at the Indy

500; Fl's Suzi Wolff; and even a female *Top Gear* Stig. All are proof that women and speed have a long and rich history. Yet even as recently as 2011, in the middle of a successful Indycar season, Simona de Silvestro was denied entry into the USA after a customs officer did not believe her explanation for multiple trips in and out of the country was that she was a racing driver.

Away from the world of motorsport and in the realms of land speed extremes, women have enjoyed a similarly restricted opportunity. One remarkable land speed competitor was Betty Skelton, a daredevil who flew an aeroplane single-handed at just twelve years old and later became the first woman to race at Indianapolis. She initially got a job in PR for Chevrolet, organizing rallies - which she then promptly entered and enjoyed great success with. She would also successfully pass the tests to qualify as an astronaut, and she went on to fly helicopters and even jets. This skill set prompted her to attempt the land speed record for women in the huge Green Monster Cyclops in 1965, which was propelled by an F86-Sabre jet engine.

The 1970s were a decade when the land speed record was exclusively broken by men, but Texan-born stuntwoman Kitty O'Neil took on the women's record then held by Craig Breedlove's wife, Lee. Kitty was half-Irish, half-Cherokee, a former platform diving champion who had been rendered deaf at five months of age following a simultaneous bout of mumps, measles and smallpox (her mother taught her lip-reading and would herself go on to co-found a school for students with hearing impairments). With her supportive mother, Kitty learnt to play the piano and cello by feeling the music through her hands and feet. She then discovered a natural ability as a diver from a young age. She was scheduled to compete at the Olympics but, after breaking her wrist, contracted spinal meningitis which at one point saw doctors conjecture that she might never walk again. Undeterred, she took up water-skiing, scuba diving and hang-gliding, telling the media 'Diving wasn't scary enough for me'. Then in her late twenties, she successfully beat cancer twice; this was clearly not a woman who was easily defeated.

She began a career as a stuntwoman and was the first to perform with the country's top stunt agency, appearing in such iconic TV shows and films as *Bionic Woman*, *Blues Brothers* and *Smokey and the Bandit*. Her success and profile were such that, in 1978, Mattel even made a Kitty O'Neil action figure. In one episode of *Wonder Woman*, she performed a stunt, falling off the Hilton hotel roof in LA, which also set a new world record for a free fall of 127 feet. She later beat her own record, jumping out of a helicopter from 180 feet. She also set the women's water speed record in 1977 at 275 mph, and a water-ski record of 104.85 mph. By now, so proficient was she at lip-reading that many people who had worked with her for years were unaware that she was actually deaf.

With all this history in mind, it is perhaps no surprise whatsoever that O'Neil would become the fastest woman on earth. On 6 December 1976, this incredible individual achieved a speed of 512.71 mph on the Alford Desert in south-eastern Oregon - raising the record from Mrs Breedlove's mark by the jaw-dropping amount of over 200 mph. The three-wheel rocket car, SMI Motivator, was powered by hydrogen to produce thrust of 24,000 lbs, said to be the equivalent of 48,000 hp. It cost just $35,000, a relatively modest amount for a 1970s land speed car. Rumour has it that she was only allowed to use 60 per cent power because of conditions in her contract with a PR company and also a toy manufacturer (legal fallouts followed). She actually travelled significantly faster, hitting a top speed of 621 mph, but after running out of fuel for the closing metres, she coasted past the line and this severely compromised her eventual average speed. O'Neil herself suggested, had she been able to use 100 per cent thrust, she could have exceeded 700-750 mph. Despite the contractual wrangles, O'Neil said the land speed runs were 'a beautiful experience'. Interviewed decades after her record speed, O'Neil was asked what would happen if her mark was eventually beaten - she simply replied that she would go out and beat it again.

Kitty always credited her diminutive frame - she was just 5'2" and 97 lb - with helping her tolerate g-forces, and went as far as to say that her hearing impairment meant she could focus on the sensations of speed more than her hearing colleagues and rivals. Talking to the *Washington Post*, this truly inspirational figure in the history of speed said, 'People say I can't do anything. I say to people, I can do anything I want.'

There are also societal issues around gender at play here. When girls grow older and are able to start racing and, later, driving on public roads, both the number of aspirational women in racing/land speed and also the opportunities available to them remains lower than for their male equivalents. From their first days behind the wheel, teenage boys are perceived to be more macho if they have a faster car. The often phallic look of sports cars mirrors the fact that driving fast is perceived as an extension of some people's egos and personality such that the faster that car travels, the more impressive the personality might be.

There are also more base factors limiting women's opportunities within the world of speed. The crudest examples might be a generation of 1970s TV comedians cracking gags about women's parking/slow driving/passenger driving etc. Women are widely portrayed in some sections of both society and the media as lesser drivers - even though surveys and studies repeatedly tell us that women are the safer sex behind the wheel. Yet patronizing slogans such as 'So Simple, a Woman Could Drive It' persisted until relatively recently. For decades, car adverts for vehicles targeting women might highlight the capacity of the boot for shopping or the space for children in the back, rather than top speed and the performance figures.

The historical bias remains substantial: Georgine Clarsen, a professor of history and politics at Australia's University of Wollongong (and herself a former apprentice motor mechanic), established that countless pioneering women were qualified as mechanics, owners of driving schools and garages, ambulance drivers and technicians, yet this contribution was often ignored, with women instead seen as passive passengers in the history of the motor car. Why is that?

There are signs of improvement in the modern automotive industry, which appears to be finally waking up to this colossal untapped potential as companies such as Daimler, Nissan, Ford and Volvo boast high-profile female designers, most

prominently with the aforementioned appointment of Mary Barra as the CEO of General Motors. During the writing of this book, there were further encouraging signs when French manufacturer Renault appointed their female finance director, Clotilde Delbos, to the role of Interim CEO.

In the fast world of motorsport, there are more specific limiting factors, not least a simple lack of opportunity. At the time of writing, there is still no woman driving in Formula 1, the pre-eminent motor race series. Yet the modern racing car is no longer a brute of a machine that conservatives might have previously suggested was 'too hairy a beast for a woman to drive'. Modern race car drivers have power assistance for

*Kitty O'Neil sets the women's land speed record in The Motivator, hitting 512.71 mph in December 1976.*

every facet of their car; on the podium at the end of an F1 race, drivers are often barely sweating, unlike back in the 1970s and 1980s, when racers might lose a stone in weight from the physical exertion of a two-hour race. Whether this precluded women from being able to drive those older, more physically demanding cars is open to debate, but surely if that were the case then why are there no women in modern Formula 1? Further, if it is physicality that precludes women from racing, how come IndyCar legend Danica Patrick won the 2008 Japan race, came third in the 2009 Indy 500 and switched to NASCAR, snatching pole position in 2013, despite being only 5'2" and 100 lbs? Also, with so much importance placed on the all-important power-to-weight ratio of race cars, with drivers under

immense pressure to maintain incredibly low body fat percentages, how is it that more diminutive drivers - perhaps female - are offered less of an opportunity? Women can't be too small to race in a sport where winning some races is heavily influenced by power-to-weight ratios ... that can't work both ways. F1 supremo Bernie Ecclestone once said that although he felt circumstances conspired against women racers, his 'greatest wish would be to find a real gem'. It seems his wish is yet to be met ...

Valerie Thompson has this to say about her own experience of gender in speed:

*Funny Cars are anything but hilarious – this monster, driven by Courtney Force, is capable of hitting in excess of 300 mph; Courtney's reaction times on the start line are famously rapid.*

There have definitely been some obstacles in place due to my gender, but that's just not going to stop me; I've climbed over them, I aspire to get better every year, be stronger, keep pursuing this big, crazy speed adventure, wherever it takes me next. Regardless of being a woman or man, we can do anything as long as we put our heart and passion into what we do.

Bloomberg writer and automotive expert Hannah Elliot has some fascinating opinions about the challenges facing women in the world of speed:

Certainly the world of speed is completely dominated by men. Yet, if I am being totally honest, in my line of work and life around speed, I have never felt that anyone has been outright negative to my face about me being a woman specifically. Of course, online and on social media is a different experience and there's certainly a negativity around speed in that domain. But in the course of my work and life, face to face with executives, motorsport people or other journalists, I have not experienced outright exclusivity because of my gender. That said, the older I get, the more aware I am of very subtle assumptions and indeed omissions that are very present that maintain the current machine of male dominance in speed. It's not overt and I don't even think for most men it's malicious, it's just the status quo and it will take a lot to challenge that. In terms of motorsport and land speed, certainly breakout drivers help, but I think what it will take is an institutional shift that's got to start with how people raise their daughters, getting young girls into karting and even just showing little girls that a life in speed is a viable option, if you want to pursue it.

Surveying the number of women who have influenced the history of speed and examining the level of their talent means there is no argument that women have not contributed to the narrative. It is more the

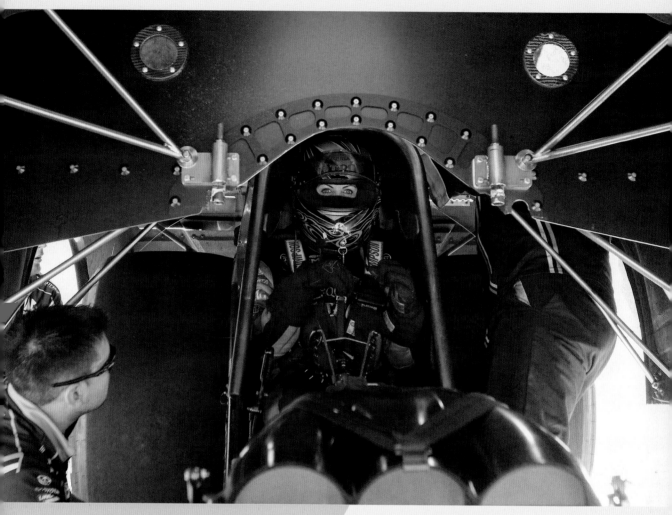

*The cramped, deafeningly loud and highly dangerous cockpit of any drag racing car is not for the faint hearted –as shown here by Alexis Dejoria in her Funny Car.*

case that their efforts have been either restricted by a lack of opportunity, diluted or downplayed by society and/or the media or even, at times, completely ignored. As this chapter has illustrated, many of the great characters in the story of speed, the most talented drivers and inspirational role models have been women, yet these triumphs have been very much against the odds. It is a simple statement of fact that women have very often been consigned by so much of the speed or automotive world, and indeed society, to the passenger seat, derided and generalized as bad drivers, ignored by car dealerships and denied opportunities in motorsport, car manufacture and auto design. The language of speed remains essentially discriminatory too, embedded deeply into accepted semantics. People talk of women drivers or women racers, rather than simply drivers or racers. If a male racing driver fails to qualify for a race, it is because his driving isn't up to scratch or the car let him down; if a female racer fails to qualify, remarks are inevitably made about gender. Until the most visible women at some high-profile races are not just scantily clad grid girls, women hoping to live in the world of speed will continue to face significant obstacles.

By way of closure, motorbike land speed record holder Valerie Thompson highlights an absolute truth in terms of gender and speed: 'My bike or my car doesn't know what gender I am; to the machines, there are no male or female world records. That doesn't matter, it doesn't even exist as a concept.'

*Top Fuel drag racer Leah Pritchett has a career high speed of 334.15 mph.*

# Chapter 19

# Hitting the Limiter?

*For Britain and for the hell of it!*

Land speed legend Richard Noble OBE, when asked why he wanted to become the fastest person on earth

As speed records evolve, there comes a point where increments get smaller and smaller, because the available technology and applicable engineering are reaching their limit. For example, drag racers can put 10,000 hp or more in an engine, but tyre technology will prevent that power being translated into actual grip; land speed cars can find huge dry lake beds to perform high speed runs, but so massive are the speeds that even the slightest issue could prove catastrophic; road-going supercars have similar tyre limitations, but are also faced with the logistics of public roads, funding and even top speed relevance ... there are many

examples. Back at the turn of the twentieth century, the land speed record would sometimes last only a few days or even hours. Then during the 1960s, Breedlove, Green and Campbell swapped the title across only a few short weeks. However, this rapidity and scale of improvement becomes inevitably more difficult as the records get higher.

Of course, achieving what is perceived by many as impossible is exactly the kind of notion that the land speed fanatics love to disprove. It was in this exact spirit that in 1983 a remarkable British car and crew was the next to raise the land speed bar. In the modern era, Gary Gabelich's The Blue Flame had held the land speed record (630.478 mph) for an impressive thirteen years before Britain finally crashed the land speed party again with one of the genre's greatest characters, Richard Noble, and his amazing car, Thrust2.

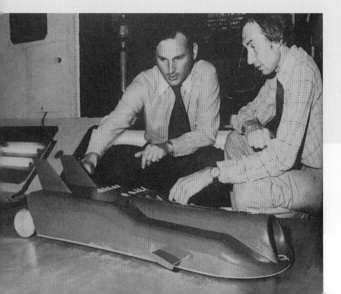

*Richard Noble OBE's personal story of land speed is a tale of individual creativity, relentless determination, a sheer refusal to quit and astonishing bravery.*

As a 6-year-old child in 1952, Noble had seen John Cobb's 200-mph jet hydroplane Crusader at Loch Ness, and that fleeting encounter changed his life. Growing up obsessed with the challenge of speed, Noble relates his vivid earliest memory:

*We were driving in my family's Hillman Minx around the north side of Loch Ness and as we came around a corner down into the little village of Drumnadrochit, on the left-hand side was Temple Pier and ... there it was, this stunning boat, looking like the ultimate racer just sitting on the pier. There was a huge crowd of people looking at it; now this was a big silver and red boat, about 30-foot-long, and it was sitting there with a Coles crane for lifting it into the water.*

*I saw this wonderful hydroplane just waiting there, it was absolutely an amazing boat, powered by a Ghost jet engine at a time when most aeroplanes had propellers. Post-Second-World War Britain was a pretty dreary, austere sort of place, there wasn't anything really exciting going on and then suddenly there was this guy with this huge jet-powered boat on Loch Ness heading for 250 mph on water – I was just absolutely obsessed.*

*We lived in Inverness in Scotland, and around the area all the shops were full of Crusader goodies: people were making models of it, everyone was really excited. Unfortunately, we weren't able to see the run itself, but 5000 people did and watched this great speed hero from the hillsides as Cobb raced across the water. Although I was so young, I got this exciting buzz from seeing the boat, and that feeling has never really left me. In fact, I've pretty much spent the rest of my life doing speed projects of one kind or another.*

*When I was a kid, I built jet engines out of cardboard and all that sort of stuff. As a youngster, I had all the books on the legendary engineers, the great steam ships and all these amazing aircraft, full of all these beautiful Eagle illustrations showing how they did it, how they built aeroplanes, how a jet engine works.*

The dream never left Noble and, much later, working a variety of jobs including overseeing £20 million of sales at ICI, he pursued a successful business career. Then, even though he had no experience of land speed itself, he decided to build his own jet car in a lock-up garage in Thames Ditton for a national record attempt. Noble's motivation to attempt land speed records shines a light on the thinking of these remarkable individuals who put so much on the line to be the fastest; his reasoning is also a throwback to the age when land speed was a national rivalry:

*Personally it wasn't for any acclaim or fame, that was no part of my thinking because it's not something I've ever craved. It was just a challenge that I was absolutely fascinated by. Just a hell of a great challenge. I come from an age when Britain was doing the most fantastic things in aviation, creating these very exotic aeroplanes like the Lightning and the Vulcan bomber, the Concorde, the TSR2. As a nation, we were actually pushing the boundaries of what was possible and solving all these very difficult engineering challenges and dealing*

*with these awful people who say, 'It can't be done.' However, with the Cold War coming to an end, that notion was getting diluted. Times were changing.*

*Prior to Thrust1, my first land speed project, the quickest I'd ever been was about 120 mph in a Triumph TR6. I had no experience whatsoever. I'd got no team, no money, but you've just got to go for it. I built it in that garage in Thames Ditton. I'd be welding late at night in the garage, the weld light flashing all over the place but gradually making progress, day after day. I funded it by selling my TR6. The next move then was to get the engine. I eventually secured a Rolls Royce Derwent 8 that the RAF were clearing out from the obselete Meteor fighters, in fact by then the Derwents were used largely for blowing snow off runways. This was a centrifugal engine, which meant that it was nice and short and easy to install, plus it didn't need a special intake and could be started by truck batteries. Ultimately the entire build took about a year, something like that, all from my garage.*

Noble called his car Thrust1 and because of its girth - decided by the wide Derwent engine - the team called it the Cathedral on Wheels. Once he had built his land speed car, the test runs were not without incident. Frighteningly, this self-built Thrust1 driven by a self-taught driver suffered a terrible crash in March 1977 at RAF Fairford in Gloucester, Britain, sending the vehicle into a series of horrifying barrel rolls at 140 mph, destroying the car but amazingly leaving Noble unhurt. Like so many land speed chasers before him,

192

Noble admitted he was planning the next step almost before he had climbed out of the wreckage: 'I was actually very pleased because although we crashed, we'd probably been quite close to 200 mph on the first run.'

The remains of Thrust1 were sold off for £175 and Noble immediately started work on Thrust2, even advertising with a short column in the *Daily Telegraph* stating, 'Wanted: 650 mph car designer', which resulted in John Ackroyd joining the team as designer . Using a Rolls Royce Avon afterburning turbojet generating 17,000 lbs of thrust (bought from the Ministry of Defence) sitting on Wolfrace wheels specially built for the Lightning aircraft tyres, designer John Ackroyd positioned the cockpit alongside the engine but also, bizarrely, boasted a passenger seat on the other side!

*The first thing we did was to put the jet car on the runway at RAF Leconfield and I drove it first at 30 mph and then at 80 mph, got out and said, 'God, that was really fast,' and the team just said, 'No, it wasn't.' At that point, Tony Meston was travelling alongside me on his bike. Gradually we got faster and faster but it was a very difficult runway to drive because there was a great big hump in the middle so you couldn't see the other end. Also, Leconfield was used for military driver training so there were operating traffic lights. You'd start off at one end, bang the car into afterburner with this huge flame blasting out of the back of the car and approach the traffic lights at 150 mph and they would go red!*

*I think I upset an awful lot of people because I wasn't very good. However, I just kept going, over and over again, and gradually got better and better. We then plugged the team into the national air show circuit and ran the car on all the best runways in Britain, zapping the car up to 200 mph, banging out the parachutes every weekend, and that was really good for practice for us all.*

Noble and Thrust soon surpassed the British mile speed record on the USAF runway at RAF Greenham Common that was only 1.9 miles long, peaking at 260 mph and averaging 247 mph for the two passes. There wasn't much room: 'I stopped the run just twelve feet from the end of the runway!'

However, Noble's eyes were on a bigger prize. After six years of his team grafting incredibly hard every day, Noble climbed into the cockpit on the Bonneville Salt Flats, Utah for the first world record attempt.

*Even then I wasn't really quite sure what I was doing. What we didn't realise was that we were making an absolutely crass mistake because the car used solid tyreless high-speed wheels but when you're running on a hard salt surface as at Bonneville, the wheels just hammer like hell on the salt and that ruins your stability and there isn't much grip. The first time I got in the car and drove, I thought This is going to be great! It wasn't. On a later run, I set off down the track, the solid wheels slipped on the salt and the car turned right and went one and a half miles into the desert and I just couldn't control it. It was an extraordinary experience because there was no feeling through the steering wheel at all, it was just dead. Eventually we realised that the car gets maximum stability when you used the afterburner. Previously I'd been a little wary of the afterburner, because the car appeared unstable and I was concerned that the massive power increase would make it dangerous. I was wrong, the afterburner actually improved the car's stability - the important thing was never to cruise the car at high speed - either accelerate hard or brake hard.*

Noble hit 500 mph at peak, but then the rains brought a premature end to his run. Despite returning home to more financial challenges, Noble was determined not to miss his chance. Further test runs included one at RAF Greenham Common that ended in a 300 mph accident with 4000-foot skid marks. It was caused by Noble's driver error.

After a number of further cancellations due to weather conditions, and with sponsors becoming restless about the repeated setbacks, in 1983 Noble finally set a new land speed record of 633.468 mph. He topped out at a high speed of 650 mph, which he reached in 59 seconds from a standing start. It wasn't just his top speed numbers that were impressive: he also recorded 9 seconds to 200 mph, 20 seconds to 400 mph, and 40 seconds to 600 mph. At this speed, Noble reported seeing a haze of condensation from the shockwave appearing in the front of the car, recounting how 'it was really something to see'. At that point, the 4-tonne, 27-foot-long

Thrust2, powered by its Rolls-Royce Avon 302, was generating over 35,000 horsepower. Perhaps even more impressively, the car proved reliable enough to travel above 600 mph eleven times. 'I loved driving that car. We'd be out most mornings doing 600-mph runs. Gee whizz, I loved it.'

Even so, the actual experience of driving a land speed record car is obviously highly demanding:

*The physical element is the acceleration. Between zero and about 300 mph Thrust2 is very difficult because the car is on aluminium wheels and it's sliding all over the place but you absolutely must not let up, you mustn't let your right foot up, you are full power all the time from the moment you start off. You've got to keep your foot down, you've got to keep the car in its 50ft wide desert lane - then once you are over 300, there seems to be some sort of transitional point where the airflow starts to really work around the tail fins and provide real stability. From about 300 to 550 mph or so, it's really rather boring, you are just going faster and faster and faster, the engine is making a terrific roaring noise and you are zipping along, you don't get time to think about it because you've got to drive this thing to the graph, you've got to deliver and the team will get most upset if you don't deliver the numbers or wimp out. At the other end of the run, when you fire the brake parachute, you get between 5 and 6 G deceleration, you are losing speed at over 130 mph a second. When you are down to about 400 mph, to be honest it is so boring that you want to get out, you want to open the car door and get out.'*

Noble didn't 'wimp out' and instead became the new fastest man on earth, yet unexpectedly, his reaction to setting the new record was not what an outsider might have imagined. After the initial euphoria of achievement, he recalls feeling 'enormous sadness. It was a very sad situation. You are like a little army, you have all fought like hell to get this thing done, you have taken the most appalling risks and consequently you have become a very close team over a number of years. Then suddenly it's over, there is no need for the team or the project any more, it's finished. So very mixed emotions.'

In a field where the maverick drivers are often highlighted as heroic individuals, Noble is at pains to disagree with this unilateral focus:

*You're asking the engineers to do something that has never been done before, you are asking them to push the limits, and yet always at the back of their minds is the knowledge that somebody has got to sit in this thing and drive it, therefore it's got to be safe and it's got to be survivable.*

*Land speed is not just about money or engineering or contacts or sponsors - the whole thing is about team. It's about a group of people who fight together as a team, survive together against all the odds. Often it's a fight against the British Establishment, against financial challenges, against all kinds of objections, sometimes going fast is one of the last things you actually worry about. You're*

*taking people way beyond their experience and their technical knowledge but also their personal knowledge of their own abilities too, and as a consequence you see some incredible personal achievements. So, it's about turning the organisation into a fighting force which can take on anything and anybody, in order to get our record. That's the thick of it, really.*

The story goes that, having broken the world record, the team sat down to dinner to celebrate with their American friends, as the first data was extracted from Thrust2. It showed that the record-breaking car was just 7 mph away from take-off. The car had reached its maximum speed of 650 mph, but the great achievement was that the car had actually achieved its design speed of the same.

Noble has one final story to tell about his remarkable time as the fastest man on earth:

*Er, yes, not long after the record was set, I was done for speeding on the M4. You are driving along and you get that awful feeling when you see the 'flash flash' of those blue lights suddenly in your rear-view mirror and you think, Oh damn. I positioned my car on the hard shoulder and got out to meet the policemen and my fate. 'Hello, Mr Noble', he said, 'Just testing, were we ?!'*

It would be another fourteen years before Noble's record would be broken, and even then he would be at the helm of the new project, if not the wheel of the car. In the autumn of 1997, Noble masterminded the barely imaginable - and still unbeaten - land speed record of 763.035 mph by the Thrust

Supersonic Car, or ThrustSSC, driven by RAF fighter pilot Wing Commander Andy Green.

This huge car sat on four solid forged aluminium wheels, and used two afterburning Rolls Royce Spey 202 engines from an F-4 Phantom, generating a colossal 100,000 hp and 44,000 lbs of thrust! Initial record attempts were ruined by inclement weather and mechanical difficulties while on test in Jordan. As a man who has broken the land speed record himself, but also shared the experience with Andy Green, Richard Noble has a unique and very interesting observation about the first time he saw ThrustSSC run:

*Seeing a car break the world land speed record is a hell of a thing, because from my point of view I had never witnessed a car do that, I had always been inside, you know. When you see a car doing 600-plus miles*

*an hour with your own eyes, it is absolutely bloody awe-inspiring, the noise, the vibrations, the senses are just bombarded.*

In a magnanimous gesture, ThrustSSC's competitor Craig Breedlove - whose own US-funded attempts had been falling short at just over 530 mph - offered the rival ThrustSSC team his slot on the desert to go for another record run.

Richard Noble remembers:

*Craig was in bad trouble because he had been up to about Mach .9 and the car turned on its side. When he saw that we had pulled so far ahead, he then realised that the gentlemanly*

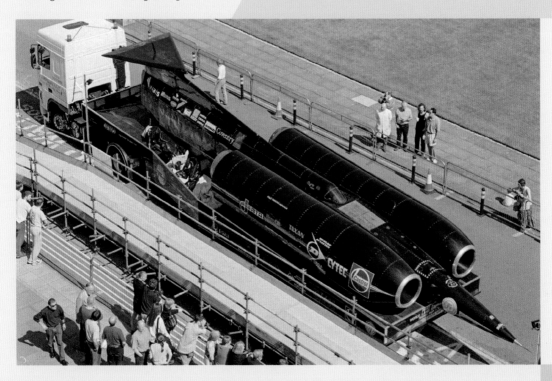

Away from the expansive desert landscapes of world record runs, when a land speed record car is seen in an everyday setting, the sheer scale and power of these astonishing machines is more obvious.

*ThrustSSC – the first car to go quicker than the speed of sound and, at the time of writing, the current land speed record holder. New land speed records are only recognised if they beat the previous mark by more than 1 per cent – ThrustSSC beat the previous mark by almost 13 per cent, adding over 80 mph to Thrust2's mark, the biggest increment in land speed record history.*

*thing to do was to give us a bit more time on the desert. However you look at it, that was very generous of him.*

Green and Noble did not waste this generous opportunity, this time taking their car past the sound barrier, at 749.876 mph and 764.168 mph; however, dismay followed when it became clear that the second run had been completed 49 seconds outside the allotted time of one hour for both measured attempts.

Relentlessly focused, Noble's team came back yet again two days later and this time averaged out at 763.035 mph, The ThrustSSC team had made four supersonic passes. In

effect, this meant that when the 10.6-tonne machine drove past at that speed, it would be passing well ahead of its own sound. Cockpit footage of this incredible achievement show Green applied extensive corrective steering inputs and skill as the car tended to drift away from the white course guide line.

Richard Noble watched on from the mid-point of the course and had his own concerns:

*Watching ThrustSSC go supersonic was absolutely bloody terrifying. I'm standing there thinking, You were the idiot who did all this, you put this damn thing together and here it is, going up and down at supersonic speeds, Andy is inside, the prospects of disaster are enormous, if something goes wrong, it's not survivable … I almost felt like I had misled all these people along the line so I really started to have serious misgivings but Andy did an absolutely brilliant job.*

The sonic boom (visible on the picture on pages 2-3) could be heard 40 miles away and even shook buildings 15 miles away. The local school had a problem because the entire building shook and the water sprinkler covers dropped into the classrooms!

The average speed was also the largest speed increment in land speed history. Andy Green remains the only human to have ever passed the sound barrier in a ground-borne vehicle. Interestingly, he did so almost fifty years to the day that American pilot Chuck Yeager first broke the same sound barrier in an aeroplane, the Bell X-1 research rocket aeroplane.

Since 1997, there have been multiple projects aimed at beating the ThrustSSC record. Craig Breedlove's car was sold to record breaker Steve Fossett but unhappily Fossett lost his life in a flying accident and the project never advanced.

One element of all this high-speed competition that is very striking is the sense of camaraderie and friendship among many of the competitors. Although these are people risking their lives to out-do each other across the deserts of the land speed world, Craig Breedlove's gesture of offering his own running time to ThrustSSC is symptomatic of this mutual respect. 'We are all sort of friends for life,' explains Richard Noble. 'If I go to California tomorrow and bang on Craig's door, I would probably be staying there for days.'

At the time of writing, there is a new British car aiming to break this record. Originally called Bloodhound SSC and again pioneered by Richard Noble and driven by Andy Green, the car actually had the 1000 mph mark in its

*The Bloodhound land speed car was the brainchild of land speed legend Richard Noble OBE, whose battles and astounding determination might best be summed up by the words of one of his predecessors, Donald Campbell:*
Every man has something to write of his struggles, successes and failures on his ascent of the mountain of progress. But each can only go so far since the mountain has no summit, for it leads to the stars. It has to be climbed, for mankind cannot regress; he may pause momentarily, but there is no going back on the path of life.

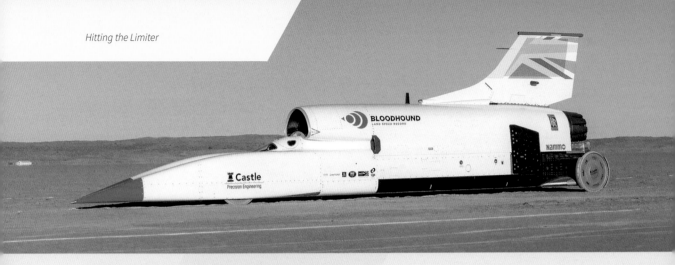

*If Bloodhound LSR manages to break 1000 mph at some point, then if there was a commercial passenger aeroplane flying on the same strip of desert, the land speed car would be travelling around double the speed of the aircraft.*

sights as an ultimate goal. However, despite massive public support and huge numbers of children benefiting from the associated STEM subjects education programme, the project struggled to find the private funding it needed to make the record attempts. In December 2018, the project changed hands and, at the time of writing, Yorkshire entrepreneur Ian Warhurst has been providing cashflow and the project is looking for sponsors. The project has two phases with distinct objectives: Phase 1: to set a new world land speed record of over 800mph; then the team will turn their attentions to Phase 2 - hitting 1,000mph!

The engineering behind such a project is truly mind-boggling: from a standing start, the car will be 12.4 miles away within 2 minutes; at a speed of 1000 mph, each mile will be covered in 3.6 seconds, at which point the wheels will be turning 10,500 times every minute, the equivalent to 170 times per second; at that moment, the g-force on the rim of the wheel will be 50,000 Gs;

the interior of the rockets will reach 3000 degrees Celsius, the same as a volcano; to cool this down, the car can gulp in 64,000 litres of air per second into the carbon composite jet air intake; and to safely prepare the surface of the track for this dazzling attempt, the project's clearance team have removed 16,000 tonnes of rocks from the Hakskeen Pan in Northern Cape, South Africa. One final startling statistic: if the car does hit 1000 mph, it will be travelling at around 230 mph faster than the speed of sound.

Land speed engineering is now pushing the very envelope of known physics, so perhaps this is why Gary Gabelich's record stood for thirteen years, Richard Noble's lasted fourteen years and, at the time of writing, Andy Green's record remains unbeaten after twenty-two years. For many, ThrustSSC's record remains the ultimate land speed record - just ninety-nine years earlier, the very first speed mark had been set by Gaston de Chasseloup-Laubat in his Jeantaud. Although the subject of much fanfare at the time, that speed was indeed slower than that of some racehorses; less than a century later, a human had passed the speed of sound in a car.

# Chapter 20

# Salt and
# Streamliners

*We weren't fooling around, we started him seven miles back.*

Mike Akatiff, Ack Technologies team owner, commenting on one of Rocky Robinson's attempts on passing 400 mph to set a new motorbike land speed record

Although this book focuses on four wheels and car-based speed, there is a world of motorbike speed records that deserves considerable attention. The land speed record for motorbikes features some astonishing machines with multiple categories, but just like the car world, there is also an ultimate top speed record. Glenn Curtiss is recognized as the first great motorbike land speed champion, using self-built aircraft engines strapped to a bike to hit speeds as high as 136.27 mph way back in 1907. This record was notable because at the time this was faster than the land speed record for a car, which stood at only 127.66 mph, set by the remarkable Fred Marriott and his flapping eyeball.

The Fédération Internationale de Motorcyclisme (FIM) was set up in 1920, a little later than the FIA, following a 104.12 mph run by Gene Walker on an Indian motorbike on Daytona Beach but, unlike the rampant setting of records across in the world of cars during this period, it was another ten years before that record was officially beaten. In these early days, BMW were the benchmark.

By the outbreak of the Second World War, the record stood at 173.68 mph, set by Ernst Jakob Henne in Germany, a BMW works rider and German champion.

After the war, other manufacturers such as Vincent, Triumph and, of course, Harley-Davidson entered the fray. The advent of streamliner bikes in the early 1950s then altered the top speeds beyond recognition; the Texas Cigar of 1956 hitting 214 mph was the first notable success in this new genre. As with the car world, the advent of jet engines changed the game, such that speeds raced towards the 300 mph mark. The first man past the 250 mph and then 300 mph barriers was businessman and racer Don Vesco. Then in 1978 at - where else? - Bonneville, Vesco powered to a speed of 318.598 mph on his twin-turbo streamliner Lightning Bolt.

The record has steadily climbed since then, and at the time of writing stands at 376.363 mph, set by the remarkable Rocky Robinson in the Ack Attack streamliner motorbike. This was a dual 1300 cc Suzuki Hayabusa Sport Bike with Garret turbocharger, which boasted a colossal 1000 hp! Rocky is a former speedway champion who has set multiple speed records. The Ack Attack parried with the BUB Streamliner team and swapped the record several times in the first decade of the 2000s. In a September 2008 attempt, Rocky's bike crashed at over 320 mph and barrel-rolled sixteen times. He emerged relatively unhurt and pushed on, eventually scooping the ultimate prize when he hit the new motorbike top speed record in 2010. The peak speed registered during the record run was a stunning 394 mph – with this fact in mind, the Ack Attack crew are determined to become the first team to produce a motorbike capable of passing the 400 mph mark.

The USA's Queen of Speed, Valerie Thompson, became the current world record holder for a woman on a motorbike, when she set 328.467 mph in 2018. After a successful career in banking, Thompson started drag racing, enjoying rapid success, and has gone on to become an eight-time land speed record holder. Like Richard Noble, Valerie's unique insights into her record-breaking run are fascinating:

*A lot of things happened in that run not many people know about, because I always just want to share the excitement. So many bad things happened inside the cockpit that I'd never experienced before. My shift light and my computer dash all went out. Also, it was so*

*Streamliner #899 is piloted by Rocky Robinson, who set the land speed record for motorbikes on 25 September 2010 at a speed of 376.363 mph on the Bonneville Salt Flats in Utah, USA. That still stands as the absolute record for motorbikes.*

bumpy, I hit my head a little bit, banging from side to side because it was so bumpy. That kind of knocked my peripheral vision out, which is so important on a record run – there are so many peripheral challenges alongside going fast. Aside from the technical challenge of driving the car or bike, you've also got to pay attention to your mile markers, they have these big clear numbers usually on both sides of the track and if you are focusing on your speedo too much and miss one of those ... then that's a big problem. These machines do not slow down too easily, they take five miles and use four parachutes to stop, so you can't be obsessing about your speed and not keeping a close eye on everything else going on around you. So when your head is being smashed around and banged inside the cockpit, that peripheral awareness is compromised. Turned out I was only running on three cylinders, I was only in third gear and the bike wasn't running properly and that's why it was so bumpy. Then suddenly my canopy button went 'pooph' like it was ready to open, but thankfully it didn't.

*Valerie Thompson and her team's record-setting streamliner bike is aiming to break the 376.363 mph mark.*

When the run had ended, first of all I unbuckled myself out of the machine and went right down on to my knees and thanked God that I was still alive. That's how rough it was. Normally when I get out, I'm a happy girl, I'm a happy dancer, no matter what the speed was, but that day was so problematic that I was happy to just get out and thank my lucky God that I was alive and well.

Valerie also makes an interesting point that although the ultimate goal of land speed attempts is to set a new record figure, the specific numbers are not necessarily so important at the time of the run:

When I'm in the moment, I don't care about the specific speed. Speed is the easy part, it's everything else that's around you that is the challenge: it could be a tyre blowout, it could be a metal part on the race track at the salt flats, it could be any number of other factors. Your mind is on other things than a specific mph number. When I glance down and see my mph, I barely dwell on it because all the peripheral elements are more important. All that matters in that specific sense is what my time slip says at the end of my run. That time slip tells the truth, the absolute truth.

*Salt flats provide an ideal smooth and (mostly) predictable surface on which to attempt land speed records.*

It's hugely enlightening to hear from Noble and Thompson what a record land speed run feels like, but what does a land speed crash feel like? After Thompson's record run of 328 mph on a motorbike, she went out again shortly after and ended up crashing at 363 mph:

*Well, I definitely had an OMG moment! Before that crash, something was telling me to not run again but I wasn't listening. We suspect that it was a wind issue that tipped me over. Whatever the cause, I felt the bike start to tip and I instantly knew this was not good. I activated the parachute, then pulled my hands in tight to my body because if you let your hands go and don't*

*brace for a crash, they will flap about around the cockpit and be broken to pieces. I don't remember flipping and going straight up in the air, I don't remember crashing upside down twice, I do remember sliding for about a mile. At the crash site, there was Maybelline red (a juicy tomato red) on the salt flats for about a mile – that's the colour of the paint on the motorcycle. At one point, believe it or not, I tried to bail and get out but my instinct said, Nope, I'm going to stay put, that's the adrenaline kicking in, I probably shouldn't do that! I didn't get freaked out, I was just calm, there was a calming effect but at the same time it was hugely terrifying.*

*Valerie Thompson's record-setting bike, Target 550 streamliner, features a purpose-designed and purpose-built turbocharged 3000 cc V4 engine producing 5000 hp; using methanol as fuel, the 1600 lb car is over 25 feet long, and has to brake using a parachute due to the extreme top speed. It will do 190 mph in first gear.*

In the same breath, Valerie pointed out that the tyres on her bike are tested to 450 mph.

Her machine's incredibly strong monocoque construction had protected Valerie from the horrific impacts and thankfully proved the theories about its safety correct - she remains the only person to ever walk away from a motorbike crash at that speed. Speaking immediately after the crash, Denis Manning - Valerie's team fabricator, owner and creator (alongside John Jans and Joe Harrelson) perfectly described the jeopardy that ultimately all land speed attempts cannot avoid:

*When you are designing a machine like this, you are overwhelmed by the enthusiasm of getting the record. The theories about how much horsepower, how much frontal area, what kind of drag, all of that, you take into consideration and you make your choices. To try to get the record. The dark side, I call it, is the part where you don't really know what can happen, if you have calamity or tragedy. Accidents are arbitrary, some slow ones kill people, some fast ones can kill people but all of this is very dangerous stuff.*

Left: Tom Mellor is a multiple land speed world record holder on his vintage, streamlined Triumph with records over 200 mph in the 1000 cc classes. Mellor makes the trip to the Bonneville Motorcycle Speed Trials on the Bonneville Salt Flats in Utah, USA, annually from Vancouver, British Columbia, Canada, roughly 932 miles towing his vintage Triumph with his vintage Rolls Royce.

Below: Larry Coleman, three-time AMA National Champion and AMA Hall of Fame inductee, one of, if not the most, successful sidecar road racers in the USA. In 2011, he piloted this Bob Bakker-built Hyabusa powered sidecar to a record of 158.161 mph.

# Chapter 21

# A Mile Every
# Eleven Seconds

*The speed of time is one second per second.*

Steven Wright

While the ThrustSSC was hurtling across the Black Rock desert faster than the speed of sound, a previously defunct French car manufacturer was just beginning to develop a new supercar that would similarly raise the speed stakes in the world of road-going vehicles. In 2005 and after a

difficult engineering gestation, Bugatti finally launched the first ever road car to boast 1000 hp, the Veyron. This quad-turbo W16 rocket came with all the ultra-luxury one would expect from a car costing over a million dollars. Its record top speed was 253 mph, but that would soon be superseded

*A Bugatti Type 57SC in front of a Veyron –
both historically important speed machines.*

in July 2010 by the Super Sport version of the car, which hit 267.856 mph at the VW Ehra-Lessien private test track.

In the wake of the Veyron's incredible achievement, some manufacturers decided to withdraw from the top speed race. However, the tantalizing fact remained that the Bugatti was only just over 32 mph away from what had previously been considered an impossibility for a road car: 300 mph.

The top speed race was not over yet. A number of brilliant manufacturers such as Koenigsegg and Hennessy threatened to beat Bugatti in the race to reach this historically significant speed milestone. Back in the heady days of Gatsby and the Charleston, speed pioneers Segrave and Campbell woke up every morning and went to bed every night craving to be the first to reach 150 mph ... then 200 mph ... and ultimately, for Campbell, 300 mph in 1935; it would take road-going production cars another 84 years to play catch up. When the moment came, it was Bugatti who scooped the accolade. In August 2019, test driver and Le Mans winner Andy Wallace took the Chiron Super Sport to a staggering 304 mph. This was the third time that Wallace had driven a car to the production car record, having previously done so with both the Jaguar XJ220 and the McLaren F1.

The level of detail required to achieve such a speed with a road-going car that can be bought - in theory! - by anyone, is astounding, and so Wallace was driving a sensational piece of engineering. Automotive calculations had long suggested that 1800 hp would be required to hit 300 mph in a road car. Andy explains how these world record speed runs have evolved since his days in the McLaren F1:

*When I did 241 mph in the McLaren, we pretty much rocked up on one day, did a few runs, checked a few things and then did the speed! With the Bugatti, it was not quite as simple as that. Firstly, a year before the top speed run there was an enormous amount of engineering going on to accommodate the speed we were after. Part of that was extensive use of a wind tunnel. However, the problem is that when you are thinking about doing over 300 mph, there are issues because you can never get up that high on a rolling road wind tunnel, even the best ones operate at around 60m/s, but the Chiron at 300 mph runs at 136 metres per second. The large gap between the wind tunnel speeds and the projected top speed has to be bridged by computational fluid dynamics, known as CFD. So you are talking about a car that is trying speeds that only computers can simulate until the actual day of the run.*

Bugatti's high-speed tests were often restricted by existing tyre technology. In previous tests runs with the Chiron's predecessor, the Veyron, some tyres had exploded after just a few minutes of use.

*The fastest man ever in a road-going car – Le Mans winner and speed king Andy Wallace.*

At top speed, the full set would need changing after just 12 minutes. Yet for 304 mph, Bugatti (and Michelin) had to create a tyre that could be sold on a road-going vehicle, and compliant with every day use and regulations. For Andy Wallace, that's putting a lot of faith in not a lot of rubber - in the case of the record-breaking Chiron, the four small contact patches of rubber that connect all that power and technology to the road is in the region of just 96 cm$^2$ on the front and 143 cm$^2$ on the rear.

Andy Wallace explains:

*For the longest time tyres have been the limiting factor for these extreme top speeds. Part of that is there isn't much call for a road tyre that can do 300 mph, but the cost of creating such a tyre is significant. Even then, this limitation hasn't just been with road cars – if I reverse back to my Le Mans days, the issue with the un-chicaned Mulsanne straight was that cars were going quicker than the tyre technology at the time could safely withstand. With the Chiron, at 300 mph there are massive centrifugal forces on the wheels and tyres and associated parts. At that speed, a tyre has to withstand a tearing force of 7 tonnes, the wheel is going round so fast that it's trying to rip itself apart.*

*Bugatti offered an excursion for owners who wanted to join the 400km/h Club, whereby their prized car was taken to the Ehra-Lessien track and they were coached at length by expert drivers on the rigours of hitting the car's top speed. The course cost in the region of £25,000 and was oversubscribed.*

*At 304 mph, the Bugatti Chiron world record car's tyres are revolving 4100 times every minute.*

It's not just the rubber that has to be perfect:

*We discovered that at the upper end of the speed range, we had quite a bit of lift on the front although thankfully not enough to cause a problem. Basically, you've got about two tonnes of lift over the top surface of the car and two tonnes of downforce from the under surface so there is four tonnes trying to rip the car into two pieces. So the structural integrity of the car has to be absolutely spot-on.*

*One of the other biggest challenges at this speed is cooling – but the dilemma is that the more*

cooling systems that are added, the more the car's weight is increased and also, critically, more drag is created. The air itself reduces the aerodynamic efficiency of the car, and drag uses up the energy created by the massive engine. The engineering catch-22 is how to add power to a car that then creates a demand for more cooling, the implementation of which creates more drag, thus slowing the car down.

Notably, at 300 mph, over 1500 hp is needed to overcome the colossal drag on the Bugatti at this massive speed. So some modern hypercars actually change shape as they get quicker, with computer-controlled systems in place to make the vehicle hunker down at higher velocity. Active spoilers can further manipulate the huge forces acting on a car at this speed, to change the

*Until Bugatti perfected the heat flow out of their record-breaking Chiron, initial test runs saw the rear of the car partially melting due to the severely high temperatures.*

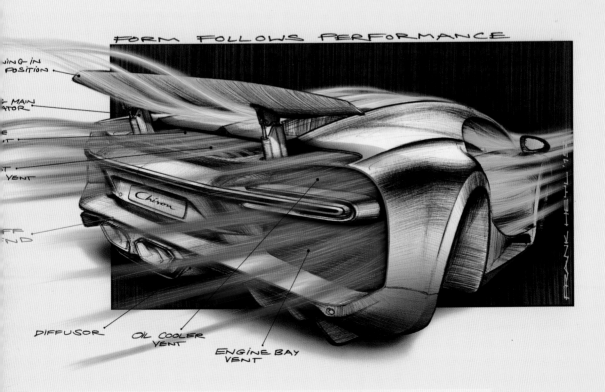

FORM FOLLOWS PERFORMANCE

DIFFUSOR    OIL COOLER VENT    ENGINE BAY VENT

aerodynamic profile. That level of precision engineering has to be equalled by the strength in every area of the car, presenting a multitude of challenges, all of which have to be resolved before the team even turns up at the test track.

Once all the engineering was complete and the car was deemed ready for the record run, it was time to head to VW's Ehra-Lessien track:

*When you get there, the first thing you do is validate all of these numbers you've got, because if you've got something slightly wrong it can prove to be very dangerous - for example, if the car was at a slightly different angle than you thought it might be, you'd basically have enough lift to fly. As a quick diversion, I have actually flown twice in a race car: once was caused by a*

*puncture, and the other one was a much bigger problem on an LMP prototype, I came over the brow of a hill at the end of a straight during the winter, but the road had sort of buckled and as I was doing around 190 mph, it touched the bottom of the car and off I took! Anyway, we didn't want that happening in the Chiron!*

*What you are initially after is a very, very low speed run to test all the aero loads out and then you measure the load on the suspension and therefore the load on the wheels and tyres at a very low speed, that gives you a baseline. You then go a little bit quicker and hold that for ten seconds, and then you measure what the load is and then you go a bit more and a bit more and a bit more.*

*The French marque Bugatti has a long heritage of combining artistic flair with shockingly fast cars.*

It starts getting a bit interesting when you are doing 250 kph, so hold that for ten seconds then you add 50k, another ten seconds, then you probably run out of space, so you come back round, you look at all the numbers then go back out again. So it's then 300 kph and then 350 and then 400 and then 450. The faster you go, generally you get more lift on the front and you get more downforce on the back. So you are watching that to make sure that when you get to roughly the speeds you think you are going to reach, that you are not going to get too much lift because then you've got a big problem. This all takes time.

In terms of the top speed run itself, it isn't just a matter of a few runs up and down the track. We weren't just there for a day; I spent a whole week there and we actually did just over 1000 kilometres of running over that seven-day period. You build up a confidence level across the week and make sure you don't take any big steps.

Hitting the 300 mph mark was very demanding, that was not easy. Part of the problem was that if we had gone close to it, smashing the existing record in the process, it would have still been a disappointment. During that week, I was building up the speed gradually but there was quite a lot of crosswind which was blowing the car around. On the Thursday, I did a 299.87 mph and several attempts to go quicker than that had to be aborted because of this horrible crosswind.

Once the record attempt itself starts, it's pretty exciting. Remember, I am trying to run a road car faster than anyone has ever done so before, so for all the testing and calculations and computer power, ultimately, I am taking a leap into the unknown. Just to throw a spanner

in the works, if you were on a billiard-table-smooth road, it might be a little bit easier. However, we were doing this at the VW test track, Ehra-Lessien, which has a 12-mile lap, a long straight and fairly high barriers each side to try and contain the car if you've got a problem. They swept the entire track to remove any dangerous debris but even then there was an issue – that track gets used a lot, 24 hours a day at times, for the testing of commercial cars. So actually the surface isn't perfect in many places, it isn't brilliant, so you get quite a bit of trembling and some bumps. A bump in the road is normally fine, but if you are travelling at 300 mph when you hit it, then that's a different story. Plus, the grain of the track is slower in one direction than in the other, which adds yet another challenge.

When you are strapped in the car and they shut the door, you are finally alone and there to do a particular job, so you take every other thought out of your mind and all you concentrate on is the job in hand. I've got vivid memories of everything on that record run because I was concentrating on what I was doing so hard, keeping the car straight, looking at the windsocks to see how strong the side wind was, looking at the GPS, there are so many things going through your mind. And despite what you might think, there is a real serenity inside that cabin. Most people are busy doing jobs and getting on with life so it's very hard to get time to ourselves, just a few moments where there are no external annoyances or distractions. There was no vibration, no noise that I could hear because I had a helmet on with radio and

*The Bugatti Chiron was preceded by a one-off design study known as the Vision Gran Turismo, created in conjunction with that game.*

earplugs, so I had no sound to speak of. I didn't hear wind noise, it was so still, even serene. When I was in the car for these speed runs (and indeed when I was racing), there is nothing else, I am totally immersed and thinking about nothing else. There is a purity of the emotional experience that is incredibly rewarding and refined.

Against that there was quite a bit of vertical movement in the car which had me bouncing in the seat, which at 300 mph can be quite disconcerting! The gyroscopic effect of these ultra-high speeds means that the tiniest of bumps can cause a surge in movement of the car. You then make a tiny input on the steering wheel but that then lurches the car across the other way, then you make another input, and another, it's a non-stop onslaught of tiny rapid inputs, you are constantly having to make micro-corrections. On camera you can't see that, but I can tell you that at the top speeds, those twitches very much get your attention. At a kilometre every seven seconds (or a mile in just over 11 seconds), you tend to notice them!

On the actual record run, the top speed was so high that the measuring technology was struggling to cope, as Andy explains:

*There is a speed radar on the straight but on the actual record pass itself, as the car flashed past, it read 502.3k mph, because it hadn't been calibrated to that speed before! Also, the telemetry signal couldn't keep up with the car, it was too fast. After I did the top speed and saw the number on my in-car display, I was on the radio thanking everybody but they were all*

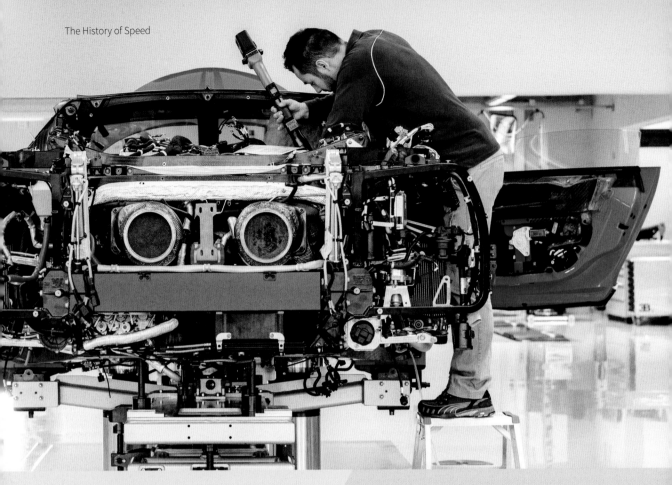

*The engine in a Bugatti is hand-crafted at their 'Atelier' in Molsheim, France, by a very small team of artisan engineers.*

*looking at each other bemused! Then, when the car came back to them and they checked, they finally realized that we had done it and so could be as excited as I was!*

Perhaps one of the most remarkable elements of this astonishing 304 mph top speed run for a series production car is that the Chiron used was equipped inside with sumptuous leather, a high-end stereo and all manner of ultra-luxurious equipment befitting such a prestigious hypercar. Apart from a safety roll cage, the removal of the passenger seat and the installation of countless measuring and telemetry equipment, the car that Andy Wallace hit 304 mph in is not so very different from one that anybody with £2.5 million could buy from a dealership.

Both ThrustSSC and the Bugatti Chiron Super Sport are astounding pieces of engineering and fully deserve to be included in the pantheon of speed records and legend. In fact, so brilliant are their achievements that they may have inadvertently hit the limiter for modern speed records. For a number of reasons, these two blistering speed records may well never be beaten. Their speed marks are so stunning, almost unbelievably so, that it will take a gargantuan effort for them ever to be exceeded. And, perhaps most pertinently, does the modern world even want that?

For starters, is there any relevance for a road-going car hitting 300 mph any more? Possibly not, although the moment supercars surpassed legal speed limits then any top speed beyond that was already effectively academic. Of course, in many senses, the notion of a top speed in excess of each country's speed limit is a nonsense. The Bugatti Chiron Super Sport is capable of exceeding the 70 mph British speed limit in first gear; if the driver is suitably inclined to risk prison, it could then go on to exceed that limit by a further 234 mph. So, in some senses, manufacturers' top speed claims are really no more than marketing hype. In the 2000s, as top speeds escalated ever further away from legal limits, many car companies began to state that their models were limited to a certain mph. In 2010, when Bugatti hit 268 mph in their world record trim Veyron Super Sport, many other manufacturers decided to withdraw from the top speed race citing it as 'irrelevant'; after Andy Wallace and the Chiron subsequently hit 304 mph, even Bugatti themselves announced that they were withdrawing from this particular game, posting on social

*The Bugatti Divo is a sports-handling version of the Chiron, intended for customers who wish to enjoy more 'extreme' driving capabilities.*

media: 'With this record set, we bow out of the race for the top speed, to focus on what Bugatti really stands for: elegance and excellence.' The marque's president, Stefan Winkelmann, endorsed this, saying, 'We have shown several times that we built the fastest cars in the world. In future, we will focus on other areas. Bugatti was the first to exceed 300 mph – its name will go down in the history books and it will stay that way forever.' He may well be proven correct – with the estimated cost of developing a new hypercar from scratch at a minimum of $1 billion, who is going to do that? With the likely next big target being 350 mph, the chances of any manufacturer having the funding to pour what might be billions of dollars, years of research/development and risk into a car capable of that number seems highly remote. Further, whether the public still retains an appetite for that to be achieved remains to be seen. Maybe, like the moon landings before them, these top speed shoot-outs have had their day?

*At the Bugatti Chiron's record top speed, an object over one and a half football pitches in length away will smash into the bonnet less than one second later.*

There is a similar challenge, albeit for different reasons, facing anyone wanting to beat ThrustSSC's achievement. Beating the speed of sound is so remarkable an achievement that future financial hurdles, engineering limits and multiple other factors might mean that the ThrustSSC has effectively ended the land speed game.

There are other reasons why this mark may be the final land speed record. Does the public care any longer about land speed record cars chasing the speed of sound and beyond? When the privately funded Bloodhound project had originally stumbled with funding, there were suggestions in some parts of the media that the land speed record had maybe had its day, that sponsors were looking elsewhere for a return on their investments and that, worryingly, the public was no longer interested in such astonishing speed attempts. Would a sponsor want to put their name on a land speed car that might take a decade to try for a record and even then potentially fail (possibly fatally so), when for a fraction of the price that same sponsor can reach millions of people in the click of a mouse? Does the social media generation retain any interest in such long-term projects when they are so used to looking at a screen, deciding whether to 'Like' an image or not, before scrolling past on to something new? Is the pursuit of speed still a human urge that will never go away,

the desire, the obsession, to be the fastest? Or is it a throwback from a bygone era? Are these speed machines now, in fact, the last of the dinosaurs?

These are just questions rather than opinions; the author's own view is very much not of this ilk. It is clearly a very subjective matter, but to qualify those fears, it is a statement of fact that if the public has finally lost interest in speed, then it would be the first time that had happened since the Jeantaud had hit a lofty 39.24 mph back in 1898. The reality may be less about public apathy and more to do with politics, climate concerns, fragile economics and the changing face of commercialism, among other factors.

For all the scepticism and doubters, you could conjecture that, were they still alive today, the Red Devil, Campbell, Segrave and Cobb would all have jumped into ThrustSSC or the Bugatti Chiron Super Sport in a heartbeat. Why? Because it is not necessarily about the method or style or propulsion for this particular breed of obsessives – it's purely about the speed.

The probability is that, as long as there are individuals who want to push the boundaries of how fast humans can travel on the surface of the earth, then there will be more land speed records and ultra-fast road cars to come ... these speed freaks always find a way.

# Chapter 22

# A Few Facts
# About Speed

*Even I can't escape my own invention, because I love speed.*

The inventor of the eponymous Gatso speed camera, Maurice Gatsonides (Having created the device in 1964 to help him corner faster when competing in rallies, he made a fortune from it, selling over 45,000 cameras to 60 countries around the world - one of which snapped its own creator breaking the speed limit.)

Society has revered and admired speed for decades. Yet speed has an ugly side. Speed on a race track, land speed on a salt lake or similar is an entirely different proposition to a reckless driver speeding along a country road or near a school in a small and unfit car. Speed in the wrong context is not glamorous; it is a killer.

The pioneers who push boundaries in land speed and road cars are acutely aware of the risks to themselves when they start a record run, but what are the issues that speed creates in the everyday world? Speed in the modern world is, of course, heavily regulated, and rightly so. For many law-abiding citizens, it will be the only time they ever contravene the law of the land. As the old adage goes, '65 per cent of people admit to breaking the speed limit on at least one occasion; the other 35 per cent are liars'. Such is the normality of speeding on public roads. Of course, there is much controversy about speed limits and punitive laws, with numerous parties and groups arguing for and against.

The consequences of excess speed - not 300 mph, but more modest speeds at the wrong time in the wrong places - can be very sinister. What is undeniable is that illegal or inappropriate speed in a public space is a major contributory factor in crashes. Speed affects a crash in three crucial ways: it lengthens the distance travelled before the driver reacts to an emergency; it affects the stopping distance of the vehicle; and it increases the energy that vehicle will introduce into any impact.

Frequently, the longer distance travelled by a speeding driver before reacting to an emergency means catastrophe is almost guaranteed. The New Zealand website arrive.alive offers some chillingly sobering statistics: travelling at the legal limit of 70 mph on a motorway, the average reaction time of 1 second will require 90 metres for a vehicle to come to a stop. That's almost the length of a football field. It means that if a pedestrian walks out in the road 60 metres ahead of a car travelling at that speed, then

*If you don't want a speeding ticket, don't speed.*

Ainsley Earhardt, US journalist

The technology already exists to constantly monitor every car via Automatic Number Plate Recognition and analyze if excess speed has been used. In theory, if a car made a journey where four or more speeding offences were committed, then that driver could lose their licence by the time they got to their destination. The social arguments for and against such policing are controversial and deeply polarized, which may explain why such systems are not yet in place.

*One wartime invention that was designed to offer protection from air raids was radar. Like many other everyday inventions created during the war, such as superglue, penicillin, photocopying and freeze-dried coffee, radar would later find a very much less militarized role in society – in speed cameras.*

however effectively the driver brakes, the pedestrian would be hit at 50 mph, with a 100 per cent chance of being killed. Even reducing the speed by just 6 mph reduces that chance of fatality by 30 per cent. In a slower environment, if a child steps off the pavement when you are 35 metres away travelling at a correct 30 mph in a restricted zone, you would stop 9 metres before the child; if you had been speeding 12 mph over that limit, the child would die.

Secondly, if a car is travelling at a slower speed when an incident occurs, then in many instances the reaction time will be sufficient to prevent any impact at all. Higher speeds mean that reaction times are severely inadequate. To put it more bluntly, a member of the public driving at 25 per cent above the average speed increases their chance of an accident by 500 per cent. And it's not just the pedestrian at risk here - the occupants of a speeding car are far more likely to die or be severely injured than those in a car travelling at a lower speed.

Third and finally, higher speed simply means more energy in any crash. Studies as far back as the 1970s confirm what many assume – that for pedestrians hit by the front of a vehicle, the injuries sustained are far worse depending on the speed: up to 15 mph, minor or no injuries are likely; at speeds of up to 30 mph, the majority of pedestrians survive; at a speed of just 5 mph more, 35 mph, the majority are killed.

In 2010, a Department for Transport report, 'The Relationship between Speed and Risk of Fatal Injury', confirmed that above 30 mph the risk of serious or fatal injury increases rapidly; at 35 mph you are twice as likely to kill a pedestrian as at 30 mph. At 40 mph, nine out of ten pedestrians will die; at 20 mph, nine out of ten pedestrians will survive. If you drive along half a mile of road at 35 mph instead of 30 mph, your risk of crippling or killing any pedestrian you hit massively increases, yet you will

*Speedometers first appeared around the turn of the twentieth century, although for many years they were an optional extra. Patented by German engineer Otto Schulze in 1902, speedometers became standard in most cars from around 1910. The old speed adage goes that 'it isn't the speed that kills you, it's the stopping too quickly'.*

get to the end of the half-mile stretch just 8.5 seconds sooner.

But why exactly does speed generate such huge increases in risk and consequence? What happens to the body in a crash at speed? This book is filled with high speed crashes by land speed and motor racing drivers, but what exactly is happening to their bodies when this occurs? The Student Edge website, in conjunction with the Transport Accident Commission, published a fascinating but frightening analysis of what physically happens in a crash at speed, and this reminds us why every road user needs to always be mindful of the everyday consequences of speed.

Driving along in a car generates kinetic energy, and if that car is brought to a gradual stop by braking, then that kinetic energy gain dissipates as heat in the brakes. However, a crash doesn't allow this dissipation to happen. The moment of impact of a crash itself lasts around 200 milliseconds; modern cars can absorb much of this energy through their crash

*A global study in 2018 confirmed what many had known for decades – that speed kills. The Paris-based International Transport Forum declared that inappropriate speed is responsible for 20–30 per cent of all road fatalities; lower speed limits led to fewer crashes and less severe crashes. In 2010, 77 per cent of all car-related deaths involved men.*

structures and crumple zones, but if the speed is higher or the crash is at a certain angle, there is only so much that any safety system can do. If the speed is modest, you may just suffer a broken collarbone from the seatbelt springing into action to prevent a much more serious injury; higher speed impacts start to break ribs, such that the faster the crash, the more ribs get broken. Beyond that, the chest loses its structure, often forcing an abnormal space between the ribcage and lungs - meaning the chest will expand but the lungs will not follow, creating massive respiratory problems. Thereafter, internal injuries can quickly become serious or fatal, with catastrophic internal organ damage. If you are not wearing a seatbelt, the consequences of impacts at speed gets really gory - the car will have stopped or slowed down dramatically but the body carries on travelling at the speed of the car before the crash, only to be stopped by smashing into the dashboard and windscreen. If you were travelling at 50 mph, then that is how fast you will hit the dash, and that is not going to end well. A renowned English plastic surgeon who specialized in facial reconstruction for child car crash victims told the author that he (gladly) retired because, following legislation to make the wearing of rear seatbelts mandatory, 'my work dried up almost overnight'.

We all know that speeding is not something we ought to be doing, but somehow there is a common perception that under certain circumstances it's excusable. Is it?

# Chapter 23

# Into the
# Line of Fire

*Racers race. Racers crave speed and the unknown. They are adventurers of a different kind and we should cherish the fact that they do this just like great artists and scientists, because we learn from them and what they do.*

Brendan Baker, *Engine Builder* magazine

When I started writing this book, South Dakota-born professional racing driver and TV personality Jessi Combs was poised to become the fastest woman ever, aiming to surpass Kitty O'Neil's record of 512.71 mph. Having spent a significant amount of time with Jessi in 2017 and remaining in touch with her since, it was unusual to have any conversation with her without hearing her incredibly energized, passionate references to going fast. An innate love of speed and her relentless personal pursuit of the women's land speed record was a frequent topic of conversation, such as at one particular dinner in 2017, when she explained how she loved speed and chatted excitedly about how going fast was an inextricable part of her life. With the latest speed attempt looming, I was very much looking forward to interviewing her for this book about becoming the fastest woman to ever walk the earth.

However, by the time I was preparing this chapter for that interview, Jessi was dead, killed in a horrific high-speed accident on the Alvord desert in Oregon on 27 August 2019. At the time of writing, the accident is still under investigation, but early reports suggest she was killed instantly, a notion endorsed by the obliterated wreckage of the jet car whose mangled debris was almost unrecognizable as a vehicle. Despite the remarkable technology and safety precautions taken by her team, and the immediate medical attention on the ground, there was seemingly no chance of survival.

Jessi's life and death are powerfully symbolic of the unique individuals who populate the world of speed and seek to push the boundaries of velocity again and again ... and again. Every speed freak, past and present, seems to have an inbuilt and irrepressible desire to keep pushing boundaries. In life, there are people who are often afraid to try something new; then there are people who will at least experiment and try everything

*Jessi Combs, the fastest woman ever on four wheels, who died during a record attempt in 2019.*

*The North American Eagle car driven by Jessi Combs was based on the fuselage of a Lockheed F-104A-10 Starfighter jet fighter.*

once. However, what differentiates speed freaks from the general population is their innate desire to push on and on ... and on. Beyond financial sense, beyond exceeding reasonable demands on their lives and work and, yes, at times beyond the parameters of what others might consider logical. As mentioned earlier, when the driver of a land speed record car starts the engine, they know that a few minutes later they will either be the fastest person ever in a vehicle, or potentially dead. Why do they still start the engine?

Born in the appropriately named Rapid City in South Dakota, Jessi's great-grandmother used to race cars including Stanley Steamers and early Volkswagens, and her family was known for its obsession with speed. 'As a young girl, there was nothing that told me I needed to do this [go fast],' Jessi explained to motor racing team Hoonigan's website.

*There was nothing that told me I should stay away from this, that it wasn't something that girls do. It was just something that I was involved with, something that I did. It was in my genes and I didn't know anything different. I just love going fast. If all I can ever do is be a race car driver, then ... mission accomplished.*

There must be something in the water of South Dakota's Black Hills, because this rural community is also the birthplace of Thomas P. Stafford, astronaut, test pilot and commander of Apollo 11 spacecraft.

Initially Jessi's interest in speed was expressed in extreme sports such as snowboarding, but she soon veered off into a lifelong obsession with creative vehicle manufacture, qualifying as a master welder, upholsterer and refinisher. In her early twenties, she would manufacture an entire car from the ground up in just six months and it was this hands-on skill set that saw her begin to pick up some high-profile TV work. It was to be on four wheels that Jessi would later make her mark on the world of speed, but in 2007 it had looked as though her future was more likely to be spent in a wheelchair than in any fast vehicle. While filming in a TV studio for a popular car show, a freak accident saw her crushed by a 550 lb industrial bandsaw that actually folded her body in two, slamming her head past her knees, critically fracturing her spine in the process. For five days, it was unclear if she would ever be able to walk again; eventually two 7-inch metal rods were inserted into her back to essentially become a bionic spine, but she would still require eight months of intensive physio and gruelling recovery before being able to walk - albeit slowly - out of the hospital.

Such a near-death experience might have encouraged a more conservative philosophy on life - not so Jessi Combs. Having been a competitive race driver in supercars, monster trucks, rally cars, hot rods, motorbikes as well as working as a stunt driver, she once said, 'I will try everything at least twice. I wouldn't want to be jaded by the first attempt.'

Jessi's list of trophies for racing is long and celebrated, but it is for her four-wheel land speed records for a woman that she will always be best known. The vehicle of choice for Jessi's first attempt? A former chase aeroplane for experimental jets, which the team transformed into a land speed vehicle with solid billet aluminium wheels. The North American Eagle Supersonic Speed Challenger was a gargantuan beast, 57 feet long and weighing in at over 14,000 lbs. And how much output was needed to get that significant mass of metal to a record-breaking speed? Over 52,000 bhp. That's the equivalent of 70 Formula 1 cars, or 400 family hatchbacks.

During the first record attempt at a dry lake, one of the Eagle's brake parachutes failed, and there were also issues with steering. Nonetheless, the team managed to modify the vehicle, reassure everyone that all was safe and ready the car for the record run. For the first mile at least, the attempt was going to plan, including an immaculate deployment of the afterburners. Then - and picture yourself in this moment - Jessi realized that at 477 mph the car was drifting left and she couldn't correct it - she effectively had no

*Jessi was renowned for multi-discipline speed wins and records, triumphing across genres as broad as land speed, motorbikes, off-road and vintage.*

steering. Realizing the serious danger she was in, Jessi triggered the airbrakes, which scrubbed off some top end velocity, but the main braking procedure - her parachute - failed to deploy. So now she had no steering and essentially no principal way of braking. Worse still, the car was veering left hard now, heading at high speed towards the shoreline. Talking to Hoonigan, she said:

*That was probably the first time that I ever thought I might not live to see tomorrow. Forty feet away [before a tranche of bushes along the shoreline] I was still going at 100 mph, yet by the grace of God something happened, the car [just] stopped before these gnarly bushes forty yards in front of me.*

More testing followed before a further attempt was made in the North American Eagle on an arid lake bed in Oregon in 2013. Speed comes at a cost – Jessi was using 90 gallons a minute at full, afterburner-assisted throttle. Concerned about the scarcity of oxygen at such speeds, Jessi wore a scuba-diving tank and mask. This time, she completed two successful runs, the second of which registered a top speed of 440 mph and created a record average of 398 mph – including maximum delivery of the afterburners, which effectively doubled the Eagle's power output to over 100,000 bhp.

'You can't get addicted to it because you can't do it often,' she continued, 'it's this unicorn that you are constantly searching for, but it is the most thrilling, amazing thing I've ever done. It's so fast, it is slow, it's so loud, it's quiet, it's so bumpy, it's smooth. You are out in the middle of nowhere and you have no way to gauge your speed.' Asked about the extreme danger she was putting herself in for the pursuit of being the fastest woman ever, Jessi said: 'All I am trying to do is go faster, to break that record.'

The day before her fatal accident on the Alvord desert, Jessi posted a striking photo on social media of her walking towards her jet-powered North American Eagle, alongside the words: 'It may seem a little crazy to walk directly into the line of fire … those who are willing are those who achieve great things. People say I'm crazy. I say thank you.'

# Chapter 24

# The Future of
# Speed

*Speed is irrelevant if you are going in the wrong direction.*

Mahatma Gandhi

It is ironic that the most significant watershed moment in the twenty-first-century history of speed started not with supercars or the land speed bullets of dried-out salt lakes, but with the reverse influence of ordinary cars adopting electric and/or hybrid technology. Many of the first generation of fastest cars in the world were in fact electric - for example, an electric-powered vehicle made by Aberdeen's Robert Anderson back in 1839 pre-dated Benz's Motorwagen by almost fifty years; Ferdinand Porsche himself was one of many pioneers

creating electric cars in the first few years of the twentieth century, perhaps most notably his Lohner-Porsche in 1898. However, the internal combustion engine soon became speed's power plant of choice, its pre-eminence even extending for many decades into the world of land speed, in addition to commercially available speed machines.

However, as discussed, although speed is a primal sensation, it is not one immune to the vagaries of society's own experiences - just as the muscle cars of the 1970s petered out amidst the oil strikes and emissions

*The 2013 Porsche 918 Spyder was one of three high performance cars in that year dubbed 'The Holy Trinity' that redefined what a modern supercar should be.*

paranoia of the 1970s, then so too has the internal combustion engine finally begun to face a serious competitor, after more than a century of dominance. The turn of the twenty-first century onwards has seen an inexorably growing unease about the continued plundering of dwindling fossil fuels, inextricably linked to the potentially catastrophic environmental impact of humankind's carbon-generating lifestyle. Inevitably, this has led to pressure on science and commerce to provide alternative, cleaner and more sustainable methods of propulsion - and the world of speed is no different. One might even question if speed itself is now old-fashioned. Is the idea of going quickly now anachronistic to the modern era of sustainability and ecological ethics?

What is perhaps surprising is that the initial impetus for this sea-change in speed's history came from everyday cars that were developed and designed with speed very low down on their list of priorities. Yet these low-speed, practical cars opened the floodgates and 100 years after electric cars lost the battle as the propulsion method of choice they are now fast re-emerging as the new kings of speed.

Initially, hybrid technology offered the alternative of using electric batteries alongside and in tandem with a petrol engine. First out of the blocks were cars such as the Toyota Yaris, Civic Hybrid and Ford Fusion Hybrid; the Fisker Hybrid was a very early foray into supercars with alternative power sources, although this car struggled to gain significant commercial traction.

Then, in 2013, a trio of supercars were launched that attracted rabid media and public attention, as well as boasting performance and speed statistics that were shockingly brutal. The history of speed is littered with new super- and hypercars being released with much fanfare, often with the tag of 'the fastest car in the world', but this trio of vehicles from the biggest and most prestigious manufacturers would become a pivotal moment in the history of speed. Known as the Holy Trinity, the McLaren P1, the Ferrari LaFerrari and the Porsche 918 truly were speed game-changers.

They each used different but highly potent methods for combining electric and petrol power; they all shared similar top speeds and 0-60 mph times; they were all priced around the £1 million mark, give or take a few thousand pounds; all three offered lower emissions, stunning performance and prodigious amounts of power; and, across a number of independently conducted road and track tests using a variety of measurements, the performance of all three cars appeared to be within 1 per cent of each other. Sold out in days, the majority before the cars were even officially launched, these three vehicles were a major moment in supercar history, and perhaps may come to be seen as holding greater significance in helping to potentially revolutionize the future of speed.

What the Holy Trinity did was instantly turn electric propulsion on its head, and consequently alter the future of speed forever. Previously, electric and hybrid cars were often derided as hippy vehicles for

people with no interest in performance, largely bought by Californian film stars or eco-warriors. However, these three manufacturers ingeniously subverted this 'new' power method for extra torque, performance and power – in essence, taking a technology intended for a more communal future and using it to make their supercars go faster. Yes, there were associated emissions and environmental benefits that came along with that, but in the reviews of these three astonishing cars, the headlines were always going to be about performance, rather than green credentials.

Even more crucially, when these cars were track-tested alongside wholly petrol supercars, with very few exceptions they proved to be quicker in almost every department. The reviews and TV analyses of this was global, and had the effect of making public opinion question its prior petrol-powered bias. Almost overnight, the Holy Trinity made people reconsider alternative

*The Porsche 918 set a lap record around the Nürburgring race circuit of 6:57 minutes, beating the previous record by a colossal 14 seconds.*

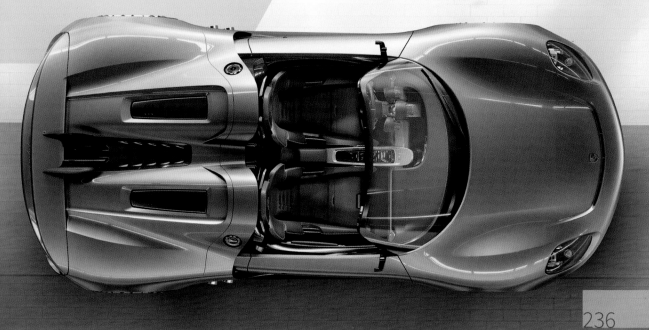

propulsion methods. Suddenly, people interested in speed were reading about electric or hybrid cars without a sneer; say it quietly, but some were even test-driving these new cars. Why? Because, despite all the headlines about global warming and the environment which justifiably and necessarily vie for our attention, the idea of a new supercar going very fast is always an easy sell. That might not be an agreeable notion, but it is a simple fact of human life. The base human fascination with speed has not decreased just because the ecological, political and social atmosphere has deemed it less desirable.

Having created some of the world's most renowned supercars - the McLaren P1 among them, as well as the Ferrari 430 and also the new Mini - designer Frank Stephenson has an interesting insight into the role that speed plays in car design:

*It's pretty much up to the engineers how fast they want to make a new car go. However, my impression with design is that a car that looks like it's moving when it's standing still is always much more interesting to look at. A fast shape looks good and dynamic shapes always tend to look better than static shapes in moving objects. Every car that I've ever designed has something to do with speed: much of the thinking behind the new Mini was based around the bulldog, it's a pretty static animal, but if you see a bulldog tugging at the leash, it is very dynamic and powerful. The Escort Cosworth had the influence from the Fokker and the speed and agility of planes; even the faster versions of the Fiat 500 had speed in mind, particularly the hill climb racers, but also how people used to leave the tailgate flipped open to keep the air coming in to the engine in the back at speed.*

If the Holy Trinity was a watershed moment when hybrid or electric power came of age in terms of public and media acceptance,

*Each of the Holy Trinity cars – the Porsche 918 (pictured above), the McLaren P1 (opposite) and the Ferrari LaFerrari – subverted innovative hybrid technology to increase performance.*

then events were soon to get even more unlikely when an American car company with no history of making vehicles turned its pioneering eye to electric cars and altered the future of speed beyond recognition. Tesla's most high-profile founder was Elon Musk, inventor of Paypal and eBay. Although one of the company's stated goals was to offer electric cars at an affordable price, for the purposes of this book it is the staggering acceleration of these cars that is most relevant, in terms of sheer speed but also the resultant public and media perception of all-electric performance.

As a start-up company, Tesla launched a premium sports car, the Roadster, and it is in this first car's performance stats that a hint of Tesla's impact on the history of speed can be found. The debut car retailed at around $109,000 on its 2008 release, yet was capable of hitting 60 mph in just 3.7 seconds, pitching it very much in among supercars from the most prestigious and traditional of marques. The digital technology inside the vehicle was

hugely impressive, but it was the instant torque and subsequent rapid acceleration on offer that piqued the interest of speed obsessives.

Tesla was not finished: at the time of writing they have a number of models, perhaps the most shocking being the family Model X. There is a widely circulated YouTube clip showing a Model X beating a sporty Alfa Romeo 4C Spider in a drag race while the Model X itself is towing another Alfa Romeo 4C Spider on a 4000 lb trailer. This was a shocking visual and real-world display of the savage instant torque that electric power generates. Other more conventional drag races have also been filmed where the same Model X comfortably beats a Lamborghini and a Ferrari; although the traditional supercars start catching up towards the end of the quarter-mile sprint, the Model X still wins by 0.5 seconds; bearing in mind it has seven seats and is an SUV not a supercar, this is really quite astonishing. If rumours at the time of writing prove to be substantiated, Tesla haven't finished yet. When fast car fanatics thought they knew and had seen everything with the Chiron, along comes Tesla with their much-hyped, all-electric, battery-powered Roadster which they claim can hit 60 mph in 1.9 seconds, the same as modern F1 cars. If reports are confirmed, then that car will completely rewrite the acceleration records for road-going vehicles. When questioned about the veracity of the speculated performance figures, Elon Musk simply said, 'This is what we are achieving in the prototype,' indicating elsewhere that performance in the actual road-going version might actually increase. Being half a second quicker (representing an improvement of just over 20 per cent) than an historically fast car such as the Chiron, which costs over £3 million, is quite an achievement, a stunning line in the sand.

To be frank, this electric evolution in the world of speed has at times made the older propulsion method of internal combustion look dated, even antiquated. Tesla founder Musk was savage in his denunciation of his internal combustion engine rivals, saying that once the Roadster is released 'driving a gasoline sports car is going to feel like a steam engine with a side of quiche'.

Further, the viral spread of social media and online footage of various Tesla models destroying famous supercars on track has pollinated this notion very quickly to a younger generation who have no loyalty to the internal combustion engine. There is a certain serendipity in the fact that Tesla brilliantly utilized the rapid digital dissemination of its brand's remarkable performance progress. These online films and clips served to market the idea of an electric car to the masses in a way that no

conventional advertising campaign could offer. Classic car lovers bemoan the loss of that sound – the roar of a Lamborghini V12, the music of a Ferrari power plant – and the visceral experience of driving a fast petrol-fuelled car. But in terms of the future of speed, perhaps this is missing the point. The younger generations who are yet to climb into a car may well be sceptical about buying what they see as a noisy, oily petrol vehicle with hundreds of parts that may fail – only for a friend in their parent's family runabout to leave them standing at the lights.

The astounding acceleration leap by this new generation of electric cars – not just Tesla's, of course – is crucial to the future of speed for a number of reasons. In real-world terms, colossal top speeds appear to now be obsolete. However, designer Frank Stephenson does not agree that road-going high-performance cars have reached their speed pinnacle:

*I don't think so, I think it's the engineering that's limiting us. We are moving into an era where we need to have shape-shifting forms on cars. We have gone from static aero where spoilers were always there, to active aero where flaps move up or down as required at certain speeds, but the next leap if we want to get serious about no limits in terms of speeds, then the shape of the car could be dictated by some kind of sensors that engage at higher speeds. Maybe that's a material that is capable of taking on different shapes as and when needed. If you can basically make the shape of the car, not just a part of the car, then there is a long way to go in terms of top speeds. At this same time, to a degree, there is no point in cars becoming ever faster at this point – at least not with the road systems we have in place. If that network changed then the speeds could increase significantly. At the moment, 100 mph on a public road is just very dangerous; autonomous cars will change that, but only if the network changes to accommodate that technology. You can't have a smart car and a dumb car competing for the same place because that can lead to problems. If you can raise the speed and compress the cars together closer … but that is a massive change in infrastructure.*

*I think speed in our society at the moment doesn't make any sense; it's like, 'My dad is stronger than your dad,' in the playground, 'I've got more horsepower than you'. At some point, it doesn't matter how much speed or horsepower you have, it becomes irrelevant in the real world, it's little more than a badge of honour that doesn't mean anything. Speed has to have a purpose, in everyday life at least, so the future technological advances must produce speed that is usable, not just for the sake of it. The whole idea is getting somewhere quicker, so speed obviously has to be the answer, you can't negate speed as an important factor of getting somewhere, but you need that in a way that is practical.*

This practical obstacle to achieving these massive high speeds already limits what lovers of speed can experience, as the chance to drive at such dizzying top speeds are effectively negligible; there are very few tracks in the world that offer this, due to the enormous distances required, and those that do exist charge a hefty premium for the luxury. For the vast majority of speed lovers, the reality is that acceleration is the buzz; that's where the masses can still get their kicks. If that is the case, then the instant torque of electric cars is a mass-market re-invention of the thrill. As hypercar top speeds have become increasingly irrelevant, perhaps electric, instant torque acceleration has just recaptured speed for the masses. Make no mistake: in terms of acceleration, the days of the petrol engine ruling the road are over.

There is a downside to this accelerative evolution. While a Bugatti Chiron at 300 mph cannot harm members of the public because it will necessarily be on a closed circuit, an electric family car that can hit 60 mph in less than 3 seconds might be another matter. With this potential danger in mind, maybe the 0–60 mph sprints of everyday cars will come under increasing scrutiny.

There is certainly no putting the genie back in the bottle – at the time of writing, pretty much every major automotive manufacturer is pouring vast amounts of money into the R&D of electric cars. Even governments are piling into the arena: in 2017, the UK government announced that purely petrol and diesel cars and vans would be banned from 2040. Whether electric, hybrid, hydrogen or some other propulsion method wins the day remains to be seen, but what is clear is that these torque-rich electric cars have certainly made a massive impact on the public's perception of, and access to, searing acceleration.

*The Tesla Roadster became the first car to be launched into space when it was carried by a Falcon Heavy rocket on a test flight in February 2019. One Tesla Roadster optional extra rumoured to be potentially available will be rocket thrusters.*

# Chapter 25

# We are
# Cars

*We've got 21st century technology and speed colliding head-on with 20th and 19th century institutions, rules and cultures.*

Amory Lovins, American writer and physicist

The impact and influence of electric car acceleration on the future of speed is clear; however there is another, less immediately obvious, development that threatens to eliminate active speed from the daily lives of everyone but the very few: autonomous driving. Einstein is oft-quoted as stating: 'Computers are incredibly fast, accurate and stupid; humans are incredibly slow, inaccurate and brilliant; together they are powerful beyond imagination.' Among the many areas of our lives that the German theoretical physicist's genius touched, maybe this idea could easily be applied to the notion of automated driving that swept the globe in the second decade of the twenty-first century. The arguments for and against self-driving vehicles are manifold and sufficiently lengthy to write a separate - and constantly changing - study. A number of manufacturers, including non-traditional manufacturers such as Google, Apple and Tesla, are aggressively pursuing the idea of autonomous driving. This is not actually a brand new idea: the automotive industry has experimented with the idea of a self-driving car from as far back as 1925, when a radio-controlled car made by Houdina safely travelled through New York. Fast-forward to the 1950s, and GM's Firebird concept car experimented with sensors on the vehicle

that would theoretically allow future travel without driver input.

However, in the modern era, although technology is supremely capable in reality, the concept of fully autonomous driving on any public road under any circumstances as a holistic, flawless model is still very much a future destination. To be fair, there has been massive progress towards this futuristic ideal – by the end of 2018, Google's autonomous car project had driven over 2 million miles under its own steam. There are also multiple signs that the architecture of travel is beginning to alter to accommodate this – at the time of writing, 29 US states have passed laws permitting autonomous cars.

This is a book about speed, not autonomous driving, but having vehicles controlled by computers to the point of not actually driving them at all means our relationship with active speed will change ... and possibly terminate altogether. If someone owns a fully autonomous car (and not a hobby/track car), then their commute becomes a passive experience, just as it would if they were getting on a train or bus. In terms of speed, projecting forward to a world in which autonomous cars are the norm, with motorways full of cars with their 'drivers' asleep or reading a book while the machine takes them to work or on holiday, then there are massive implications for the human relationship with speed. In theory, speeding fines would be obsolete, because no

manufacturer would programme a car that was capable of speeding, due to the liabilities that might create. Although electric cars have savage torque acceleration, maybe even more legal paranoia would also reduce that particular performance asset to a more mundane, gradual and safe level. Certainly, no cars would boast a top speed of more than the legal limit, again because of the risk that the manufacturer might be held liable. Designer Frank Stephenson suggests that in an autonomous driving future, maybe we need to have a recalibration of the speed limits because these self-driving cars will be able to safely hit much higher speeds; if that happens, then we may actually be entering a new era of speed.

In author Enda Duffy's work, *The Speed Handbook*, he considers that speed revolutionized space and liberation, and because it was eventually available on a mass scale, this revolution was global. He suggests that at the moment the world was finally mapped and known to be finite, speed offered individuals the opportunity to expand their world, to reduce the scale of this space. For example, people might comment that a certain town was four hours away, rather than specifying the distance in miles; increasing speeds reduced the former number, but not the second. The potential for the future of speed to repeat this feat is a point that Frank Stephenson makes:

*Technology will be able to harness speed in a safer way and in so doing increase its general* use in daily life. Most of us have a radius around our daily life that we operate in most of the time, and speed allows that to reduce, in relative terms, because we can reach the edge of that radius quicker.

Le Mans winner and speed record holder Andy Wallace has some enlightened views on the future of speed:

*It won't be autonomy that stops speeding, I think, before that, cars won't be able to speed anyway because they will be GPS-limited on their speed. To be honest, I'd be a massive fan of no car being physically able to exceed 30 mph in a city anywhere. Technology should intervene on the reckless use of speed. Around pedestrians, schools, towns and villages, there is no reason to have cars capable of going much faster, it's just too dangerous. You sometimes hear people saying, 'Oh, but 30 mph doesn't feel very fast,' but the simple fact is, it feels fast to the person that your car hits.*

If this autonomous world of self-driving cars and electric/hybrid/other-propelled vehicles comes to fruition, then where will people get their speed thrills? And will this lack of an active experience of speed in society increase the desire for something that will come to be seen as forbidden, or will it simply fade away as an outdated and antiquated impulse? If this utopian (to some) vision of transport is realized, then the speedhunters will surely be pushed ever more back to the off-road tracks, dusty private roads and perhaps even the illegal, late-night road races of yesteryear. Will the fastest cars in the world

be permanently kept under silk sheets in hermetically sealed private garages while the arteries of the world's cities are awash with homogenized, controlled, identikit forms of individual and mass transport? Is speed as a commercial entity about to be made obsolete? If, as Aldous Huxley once said, 'speed provides the only genuinely modern pleasure' but zeros and ones remove that experience, where will that leave us?

Even allowing for the reservations expressed above, there is no suggestion that speed will stop evolving – technology ensures that progress will be relentless. The point is that speed will have to mutate in terms of how it is used, where and when. Whatever your opinions on the future of moving fast, it is clear that the progress of speed chronicled in this book has itself been rapid. Should you have a spare £2.5 million and a private race track long enough (plus a good degree of nerve!), you too can buy a Bugatti Chiron – complete with luxurious interior, high-tech stereo system, heated seats etc – and in theory hit the same magical 300 mph that the land speed kings such as Campbell and Segrave had deemed so challenging decades before.

To look at the same point another way, when you're abiding by the motorway speed limit in Britain at 70 mph, sitting comfortably in a standard car with no remarkable features whatsoever, you are in fact travelling faster than any human had ever gone in a car, back at the turn of the twentieth century.

Is that quick enough for you?

*The first ever production road car to reach 300mph, the Bugatti Chiron.*

# Index

# Acknowledgements

A huge thanks to Richard Noble OBE for his interview and also for providing the Foreword – but most of all, for being the personification of what 'speed', bravery and relentless determination represents.

Special thanks to Ian Marshall at Simon & Schuster for believing in this project; also, sincere thanks to Laura Nickoll for her brilliant and precise work, and to the designer, Keith Williams. Big thanks to Carol Neath for her usual behind-the-scenes skills and support. Extra special thanks to Jessi Comb's mum, Nina.

The author would like to thank (in alphabetical order) the following people who gave freely of their time and expertise to interview for this book:

| | |
|---|---|
| Hannah Elliott | Dr Kerry Spackman |
| Don Macpherson | Frank Stephenson |
| Nigel Mansell | Valerie Thompson |
| John Morrison | Andy Wallace |
| Gordon Murray | Neil Waterman |

The following people were also instrumental in helping this project:

| | |
|---|---|
| Tim Bravo | Liam Howlett |
| Paul Chadderton | Jason Jenner |
| Richard Charlesworth | Liz Moore |
| Gordon Cottrell | Mick and Ben Pacey |
| David Coulthard | Ant Partridge |
| Nina Darrington | Kate Pool |
| Brian Davies | Peter Read |
| Trevor Dunmore | Peter Saywell |
| Rob Durrant | Wolfgang Schreiber |
| Craig Fraser | James Sherratt |
| Scooter Grubb | Simon Thornley |
| Jo Hassall | Jeremy Vaughan |
| Gerhard Heidbrink | Magnus Walker |
| Steve Higgins | and Yoda |
| Keith Holland | Keith Zanghi |

Also thanks to:

| | |
|---|---|
| Bentley Motors Ltd | McLaren |
| Bugatti | Porsche |
| Lamborghini | Royal Automobile Club |

# Recommended Reading

There are some fantastic books on the subject that are worth exploring, in no particular order:

### Expert Speed Record Books

*Thrust*, Richard Noble, Partridge, 1998

*The Fastest Man on Earth*, David Tremayne, 633 Club, 1986

*Land Speed Records*, Don Wales, Shire Publications, 2018

*The Bluebird Years*, Arthur Knowles with Graham Beech, Sigma Leisure, 1967 & 2001

*Little Book of Land Speed Records*, Liam McCann, Demand Media, 2015

*The Fastest Men on Earth*, Peter J.R. Holthusen, Sutton, 1999

*The Fast Set*, Charles Jennings, Abacus, 2004

*Speed Duel*, Samuel Hawley, Firefly, 2010

*The World Water Speed Record*, Roy Calley, Amberley, 2014

### Two brilliant books on the subject of gender and speed:

*Women at the Wheel*, Katherine J. Parkin, Penn, 2017

*Fast Ladies*, Jean-Francois Bouzanquet, Veloce, 2009

### General Motoring History

*The Speed Handbook*, Enda Duffy, Duke, 2009

*The Dawn of Motoring*, Mercedes Benz, 1986

*0-60 in 120 Years*, Keith Ray, The History Press, 2014

*Car: The Evolution of the Motorcar*, Rod Green, Andre Deutsch, 2012

*Drive*, Dorling Kinderlsey, 2018

*The Life of the Automobile*, Steven Parissien, Atlantic Books, 2014

# Picture Credits

All images are from the author's archive, except the following:

t = top; b = bottom. Pg 2-3 Richard Meredith-Hardy; Pg 5 Jessi Combs is reunited with her 2012 Triumph Bonneville following a custom rebuild by Triumph of Westchester after an accident in 2014. Photo: © Triumph Motorcycles; Pg 6-7 Shutterstock / Photomontage; Pg 9 Shutterstock / ANL; Pg 17, 18 © Daimler AG, Mercedes-Benz Classic; Pg 21 Alamy Stock Photo / Chronicle; Pg 22-23 Porsche; Pg 26-27 Alamy Stock Photo / Heritage Image Partnership Ltd; Pg 28-29 Getty Images / Hulton Archive; Pg 32-43 all Courtesy of RAC Heritage Collections; Pg 44-45, 46 and 47 Bentley Motors Ltd; Pg 48-49 Bugatti Atuomobiles S.A.S.; Pg 50 Mary Evans Picture Library; Pg 52-53 Getty Images / Apic; Pg 54-55 Getty Images / Heritage Images; Pg 56-57 Getty Images / MacGregor; Pg 58 Getty Images / Topical Press Agency; Pg 59 Shutterstock / Daily Mail; Pg 60-61 Alamy Stock Photo / Heritage Image Partnership Ltd; Pg 61 Alamy Stock Photo / Heritage Image Partnership Ltd; Pg 63 Getty Images / RacingOne; Pg 65 Getty Images / Hulton Deutsch; Pg 66 PA Images / EMPICS Sport / S&G and Barratts; Pg 66-67 Brgeman Images / © Look and Learn; Pg 68 Arthur Benjamins, www.1pilgrimstudio.com; Pg 69 Alamy Stock Photo / John Frost Newspapers; Pg 70 Getty Images / The Print Collector; Pg 72 Alamy Stock Photo / John Frost Newspapers; Pg 75 Getty Images / Underwood Archives; Pg 76-77 Getty Images / Bettmann; Pg 79 Getty Images / Popperfoto; Pg 80 Getty Images / David Savill; Pg 82-83 Getty Images / ullstein bild; Pg 85 Alamy Stock Photo / The Print Collector; Pg 88 Getty Images / Klemantaski Collection; Pg 90 Shutterstock / Frank Monaco; Pg 91 © Henry Grant Collection / Museum of London; Pg 92 Mirrorpix/Daily Mirror Thursday February 9, 1961; Pg 94 Hot Rod Magazine, January 1948; Pg 95 Getty Images / Ralph Crane; Pg 96 Getty Images / The Enthusiast Network; Pg 97 Getty Images / Ralph Crane; Pg 98 Getty Images / Loomis Dean; Pg 99, 100 Gordon Murray Design; Pg 103 Getty Images / Jon Brenneis; Pg 105 Getty Images / Popperfoto; Pg 106 Getty Images / Bettmann; Pg 107 Getty Images / Popperfoto/Rolls Press; Pg 108 Alamy Stock Photo / Heritage Image Partnership Ltd; Pg 110 Getty Images / Paul Slade; Pg 111 Getty Images / Eric Schweikardt; Pg 112-113 Automobili Lamborghini SpA; Pg 114-117 all © Daimler AG, Mercedes-Benz Classic; Pg118-119 Automobili Lamborghini SpA; Pg 120 Martin Goddard at www.martyngoddard.com; Pg 121 Getty Images / Martyn Lucy; Pg 122-123 Shutterstock / Moviestore; Pg 124 Alamy Stock Photo / Everett Collection Inc; Pg 125t Getty Images / Movie Poster Image Art; Pg 125b Shutterstock / Kobal/Aip; Pg 126-127 Shutterstock / Kobal/Paramount/Oakhurst Productions; Pg 129 Shutterstock / David Huntley Creative; Pg 131 Getty Images / George Rinhart; Pg 135 Alamy Stock Photo / Keystone Press; Pg 136-137 Hugh Moore https://www.flickr.com/photos/vehicular/149329520/sizes/l/; Pg 137 Getty Images / Fairfac Media Archives; Pg 138-139 Motorsport Images; Pg 142-143 Porsche; Pg 144-145 © Ferrari S.p.A.; Pg 149, 150 Lou Fischer; Pg 152, 153 John Townsend ©grandpriximages; Pg 158 Getty Images / Maurice Hibberd; Pg 159 Getty Images / Keystone; Pg 160 Bugatti Automobiles S.A.S.; Pg 161 Lou Fischer; Pg 162-163 Shutterstock / AP; Pg 164-165 Alamy Stock Photo / Tom Mareschal; Pg 165 Alamy Stock Photo / Tony Lockhart; Pg 168-169 Alamy Stock Photo / Patrick Barron; Pg 170-171 Scooter Grubb; Pg 173 Alamy Stock Photo / Art Collection 3; Pg 174 Alamy Stock Photo / Heritage Image Partnership Ltd; Pg 177 Getty Images / Imagno; Pg 178 General Motors LLC; Pg 180 Alamy Stock Photo / Everett / CSU Archives; Pg 181 Shutterstock / AP; Pg 182 Normal Blake; Pg 185 mediadrumimages.com / Incredible Features; Pg 186-187 and 188 Getty Images / Icon Sportswire; Pg 189 Getty Images / Andy Cross; Pg 190 British Aerospace; Pg 191 Scooter Grubb; Pg 196 Shutterstock; Pg 197 Shutterstock / AP/Dusan Vranic; Pg 198 Getty Images / Carl Court; Pg 199 Rupert Bryce-Morris; Pg 201 Courtesy of Mike Akatiff and TOP1 Oil Products Co.; Pg 202 Scooter Grubb; Pg 203 Alamy Live News / Action Plus Sports; Pg 204t, b, Lou Fischer; Pg 206, 207 Scooter Grubb; Pg 208-220 all Bugatti Automobiles S.A.S.; Pg 223 Science Photo Library / TRL Ltd; Pg 224 Alamy Stock Photo / Simon Dack; Pg 225 SWNS; Pg 226 Shutterstock / EPA / Bernd Thissen; Pg 229 David Cohn; Pg 230 Gordon Cottrell; Pg 232 Photo © Eric Wittler, courtesy www.landspeed.com; Pg 232-233 David Cohn; Pg 234-235 Porsche; Pg 236 Porsche; Pg 237 McLaren Automotive; Pg 238 Porsche AG; Pg 239 McLaren Automotive; Pg 241 Tesla Inc; Pg 242-243 McLaren Automotive; Pg 246-247 Bugatti Automobiles S.A.S. Every effort has been made to find and credit the copyright holders of images in this book. We will be pleased to rectify any errors or omissions in future editions.

First published in Great Britain by Simon & Schuster UK Ltd, 2020

1 3 5 7 9 10 8 6 4 2

Simon & Schuster UK Ltd
1st Floor
222 Gray's Inn Road
London WC1X 8HB

www.simonandschuster.co.uk
www.simonandschuster.com.au
www.simonandschuster.co.in

Simon & Schuster Australia, Sydney

Simon & Schuster India, New Delhi

Editorial Director: Ian Marshall
Design: Keith Williams, sprout.uk.com
Project Editor: Laura Nickoll
Picture Researcher: Liz Moore

A CIP catalogue record for this book is available from the British Library

Hardback ISBN: 978-1-4711-8932-6
Ebook ISBN: 978-1-4711-8933-3

Printed in China